Utopianism: A Very Short Introduction

VERY SHORT INTRODUCTIONS are for anyone wanting a stimulating and accessible way into a new subject. They are written by experts, and have been translated into more than 45 different languages.

The series began in 1995, and now covers a wide variety of topics in every discipline. The VSI library now contains over 500 volumes—a Very Short Introduction to everything from Psychology and Philosophy of Science to American History and Relativity—and continues to grow in every subject area.

Titles in the series include the following:

AFRICAN HISTORY John Parker and
    Richard Rathbone
AGEING Nancy A. Pachana
AGNOSTICISM Robin Le Poidevin
AGRICULTURE Paul Brassley and
    Richard Soffe
ALEXANDER THE GREAT
    Hugh Bowden
ALGEBRA Peter M. Higgins
AMERICAN HISTORY Paul S. Boyer
AMERICAN IMMIGRATION
    David A. Gerber
AMERICAN LEGAL HISTORY
    G. Edward White
AMERICAN POLITICAL
    HISTORY Donald Critchlow
AMERICAN POLITICAL PARTIES
    AND ELECTIONS L. Sandy Maisel
AMERICAN POLITICS
    Richard M. Valelly
THE AMERICAN PRESIDENCY
    Charles O. Jones
AMERICAN SLAVERY
    Heather Andrea Williams
THE AMERICAN WEST Stephen Aron
AMERICAN WOMEN'S HISTORY
    Susan Ware
ANAESTHESIA Aidan O'Donnell
ANARCHISM Colin Ward
ANCIENT EGYPT Ian Shaw
ANCIENT GREECE Paul Cartledge
THE ANCIENT NEAR EAST
    Amanda H. Podany
ANCIENT PHILOSOPHY Julia Annas

ANCIENT WARFARE Harry Sidebottom
ANGLICANISM Mark Chapman
THE ANGLO-SAXON AGE John Blair
ANIMAL BEHAVIOUR
    Tristram D. Wyatt
ANIMAL RIGHTS David DeGrazia
ANXIETY Daniel Freeman and
    Jason Freeman
ARCHAEOLOGY Paul Bahn
ARISTOTLE Jonathan Barnes
ART HISTORY Dana Arnold
ART THEORY Cynthia Freeland
ASTROPHYSICS James Binney
ATHEISM Julian Baggini
THE ATMOSPHERE Paul I. Palmer
AUGUSTINE Henry Chadwick
THE AZTECS David Carrasco
BABYLONIA Trevor Bryce
BACTERIA Sebastian G. B. Amyes
BANKING John Goddard and
    John O. S. Wilson
BARTHES Jonathan Culler
BEAUTY Roger Scruton
THE BIBLE John Riches
BLACK HOLES Katherine Blundell
BLOOD Chris Cooper
THE BODY Chris Shilling
THE BOOK OF MORMON
    Terryl Givens
BORDERS Alexander C. Diener and
    Joshua Hagen
THE BRAIN Michael O'Shea
THE BRICS Andrew F. Cooper
BRITISH POLITICS Anthony Wright

Lyman Tower Sargent

UTOPIANISM

A Very Short Introduction

OXFORD
UNIVERSITY PRESS

OXFORD

UNIVERSITY PRESS

Great Clarendon Street, Oxford ox2 6DP

Oxford University Press is a department of the University of Oxford.
It furthers the University's objective of excellence in research, scholarship,
and education by publishing worldwide in

Oxford New York

Auckland Cape Town Dar es Salaam Hong Kong Karachi
Kuala Lumpur Madrid Melbourne Mexico City Nairobi
New Delhi Shanghai Taipei Toronto

With offices in

Argentina Austria Brazil Chile Czech Republic France Greece
Guatemala Hungary Italy Japan Poland Portugal Singapore
South Korea Switzerland Thailand Turkey Ukraine Vietnam

Oxford is a registered trade mark of Oxford University Press
in the UK and in certain other countries

Published in the United States
by Oxford University Press Inc., New York

British Library Cataloguing in Publication Data

Data available

Library of Congress Cataloging in Publication Data

Data available

Typeset by SPI Publisher Services, Pondicherry, India
Printed in Great Britain by
Ashford Colour Press Ltd, Gosport, Hampshire

ISBN 978-0-19-957340-0

To Evan, Jennifer, Ian, and Kieran

Contents

Contents

List of illustrations

Introduction

Dreams are the fire in us.

(Marge Piercy)

A map of the world that does not include Utopia is not worth even glancing at, for it leaves out the one country at which Humanity is always landing. And when Humanity lands there, it looks out, and, seeing a better country, sets sail. Progress is the realization of utopias.

(Oscar Wilde)

The last thing we really need is more utopian visions.

(Immanuel Wallerstein)

So this is utopia,
Is it? Well –
I beg your pardon;
I thought it was Hell

(Max Beerbohm)

An acre in Middlesex is better than a principality in
Utopia. The smallest actual good is better than the most
magnificent promises of impossibilities.

(Thomas Babington Macauley)

Les utopies ne sont souvent que des verités prématurées.
[Utopias are often only premature truths.]

(Alphonse Marie Louis de Prat de Lamartine)

The word 'utopia' was coined by Thomas More (1478–1535) as the
name of the imaginary country he described in his short 1516 book
written in Latin and published as *Libellus vere aureus nec minus
salutaris quam festivus de optimo reip[ublicae] statu, deq[ue]
noua Insula Vtopia* (*Concerning the Best State of a Commonwealth
and the New Island of Utopia. A Truly Golden Handbook No Less
Beneficial Than Entertaining*), and now known as *Utopia*. The
word is based on the Greek *topos* meaning place or where, and 'u'
from the prefix 'ou' meaning no or not. But in 'Six Lines on the
Island of Utopia', More gives the reader a poem that calls Utopia
'Eutopia' (Happy Land, or good place). As a result, the word
'utopia', which simply means no place or nowhere, has come to
refer to a non-existent good place.

While most educated people in the 16th century read Greek and
Latin, the word 'utopia' quickly entered other European languages,
with the book being published in German in 1524, Italian in 1548,
and French in 1550. Because More opposed translation into
English, the book was not available in English until 1551, when
it was translated by his son-in-law.

In *Utopia*, More depicted a ship discovering an unknown island,
which has established a society based on far-reaching equality but
under the authority of wise, elderly men. It is hierarchical and
patriarchal; it has very strict laws with harsh punishments; and it
provides a much better life for its citizens than was available to the

1. Thomas More (1478–1535) was an English lawyer, politician, and author remembered as a prominent Renaissance humanist and an opponent of the Protestant Reformation. He was knighted by Henry VIII for his services to the crown, and executed for refusing to give his oath supporting Henry VIII as head of the church in England. He was canonized by the Roman Catholic Church in 1935. His most famous book was his *Utopia* (1516). This famous portrait of More was painted by Hans Holbein the Younger (c. 1498–1543) in 1527

citizens of England at the time. These are the characteristics of a utopia. They tell stories about good (and later bad) places, representing them as if they were real. Thus they show people going about their everyday lives and depict marriage and the family, education, meals, work, and the like, as well as the political and economic systems. It is this showing of everyday life transformed that characterizes a utopia, and utopianism is about just that transformation of the everyday.

While the word 'utopia' was coined by More, the idea already had a long and complex history. Utopias have been discovered that were written well before More invented the word, and new words have been added to describe different types of utopias, such as 'dystopia' meaning bad place, which, as far as we know, was first used in 1747 by Henry Lewis Younge (b. 1694) in his *Utopia: or, Apollo's Golden Days* and has become standard usage. And to call something 'utopian' has, from very early on, been a way of dismissing it as unrealistic.

People have always been dissatisfied with the conditions of their lives and have created visions of a better and longer life and hoped for a continued and improved existence after death. And at some point, some worried about the possibility of a worse existence after death, thinking that however bad this life was, it could be worse. Thus, the first great division in utopianism, between the better and the worse, emerged very early on.

We can never know when someone first dreamed of a better life but must rely on when different individuals in different cultures first wrote down a version that has survived, and such visions occur in the earliest written records we have, such as a Sumerian clay tablet from 2000 BCE. The earliest utopias were very like dreams, completely out of human control, something that would come about naturally or because some god willed it.

All utopias ask questions. They ask whether or not the way we live could be improved and answer that it could. Most utopias compare life in the present and life in the utopia and point out what is wrong with the way we now live, thus suggesting what needs to be done to improve things.

As with most topics, there are definitional disagreements. One issue that regularly confuses people stems from the failure to make the distinction between utopianism as a general category and the utopia as a literary genre. Thus, utopianism refers to the dreams and nightmares that concern the ways in which groups of people arrange their lives and which usually envision a radically different society from the one in which the dreamers live. And utopianism, unlike much social theory, focuses on everyday life as well as matters concerned with economic, political, and social questions.

The range of the word can be seen in the description by the Polish philosopher Leszek Kolakowski (1927–2009) of the process by which a word that

> emerged as an artificially concocted proper name has acquired, in the last two centuries, a sense so extended that it refers not only to a literary genre but to a way of thinking, to a mentality, to a philosophical attitude, and is being employed in depicting cultural phenomena going back into antiquity.

Here Kolakowski demonstrates the complexity of utopianism as it has evolved. I have called utopianism 'social dreaming'. The sociologist Ruth Levitas (b. 1949) calls it 'the desire for a better way of being', with the utopia as an aspect of the 'education of desire'. Within these broad categories are what I call 'the three faces of utopianism' – the literary utopia, utopian practice, and utopian social theory. And, as the quotations at the head of the chapter make clear, the word has come to mean different things to different people.

Scholars today generally use one of two quite similar definitions for the literary utopia: the first is the literary theorist Darko Suvin's (b. 1930), the second mine:

> The verbal construction of a particular quasi-human community where sociopolitical institutions, norms and individual relationships are organised according to a more perfect principle than in the author's community, this construction being based on estrangement arising out of an alternative historical hypothesis.

> A non-existent society described in considerable detail and normally located in time and space. In standard usage utopia is used both as defined here and as an equivalent for eutopia or a non-existent society described in considerable detail and normally located in time and space that the author intended a contemporaneous reader to view as considerably better than the society in which that reader lived.

Since writers of utopias keep inventing new forms for the presentation of their ideas, any definition must have somewhat porous boundaries, and contemporary utopias do not all look like what we previously called a utopia. In particular, they are more complex, less certain of their proposals, and intended for flawed humanity.

Utopian practice includes what are now most often called intentional communities, or communes, but were once called by many other things, including utopian communities, utopian experiments, and practical utopias. Here, there is no agreed-upon definition, but many scholars use mine, often with minor variations, which states that

> an intentional community is a group of five or more adults and their children, if any, who come from more than one nuclear family and who have chosen to live together to enhance their shared values or for some other mutually agreed upon purpose.

At one time, utopian practice was generally limited to such communities, but because the word 'utopia' is now used as a label for many types of social and political activity intended to bring about a better society and, in some cases, personal transformation, it is a broader category than it used to be. And all utopian practice is about the actual rather than the fictional transformation of the everyday. People joining intentional communities choose to experiment with their own lives, as do, in different ways, those who participate in other forms of utopian practice.

Utopian social theory includes: utopia as a method of analysis; the relationship between utopia and ideology first outlined by the social theorist Karl Mannheim (1893–1947) in 1929 and used by others in various ways since then; the ways in which utopianism has been used to explain social change by thinkers like the German Marxist philosopher Ernst Bloch (1885–1977) and the Dutch sociologist Frederick L. Polak (1907–85); the role of utopianism in religion, particularly in Christian theology, in which it has been seen as variously heretical and essential; the role of utopianism in colonialism and postcolonialism; and the debates between globalizers and anti-globalizers. All of these approaches are considered in this book.

Utopianism and intentional communities are complex phenomena with long histories occurring in many different settings. As a result, they differ radically from time to time and place to place. Definition at a level of generalization that would capture everything may be a useful starting point but would tell us little about the actual phenomena as they occur. Thus we need to characterize the various sub-categories appropriately so that we both capture the connections and recognize the differences. And in particular, any discussion of intentional communities must be aware that every community has its own life cycle beginning with visions and pre-planning to birth, growth, maturation, and, often, death, with death possible at any point in a community's life.

And there can be fundamental disagreements over what constitutes a good place. The classic 20th-century case is psychologist B. F. Skinner's (1904–90) *Walden Two* (1948), a novel describing a small community that had been established by a behavioural psychologist, which many saw as clearly a good place and even a guide to the ideal intentional community. Some communities were founded on this model and some of those still exist. Others read the novel as a picture of a totalitarian society. And communities are perceived differently by those observing them from the outside and those living in them, and such perceptions change as the communities and the people change. For example, intentional communities are often seen as wonderful places to be a child and terrible places to be a teenager.

Literary utopias have at least six purposes, although they are not necessarily separable. A utopia can be simply a fantasy, it can be a description of a desirable or an undesirable society, an extrapolation, a warning, an alternative to the present, or a model to be achieved. And the intentional community as utopia adds a seventh purpose, to demonstrate that living a better life is possible in the here and now. The utopian views humanity and its future with either hope or alarm. If viewed with hope, the result is usually a utopia. If viewed with alarm, the result is usually a dystopia. But basically, utopianism is a philosophy of hope, and it is characterized by the transformation of generalized hope into a description of a non-existent society. Of course, hope can often be nothing more than a rather naive wish-fulfilment, such as in some fairy tales (albeit most fairy tales turn into dystopias if carefully analysed). On the other hand, hope is essential to any attempt to change society for the better. But this raises the possibility of someone attempting to impose their idea of what constitutes a desirable future on others who reject it. Utopians are always faced with this dilemma when they attempt to move their dream to reality – is their dream compatible with the imposition of their dream; can freedom be achieved through unfreedom, or equality through inequality?

There are good reasons for both the negative and the positive evaluations of utopianism reflected in the quotations at the beginning of this introduction, and those reasons are explored throughout the book. In the 20th century, negative evaluations were strong as a result of attempts to impose a specific version of the good life, particularly Communism in the Soviet Union, China, and elsewhere, but also including National Socialism in Germany and the Taliban version of Islamism in Afghanistan. Others have seen utopianism positively as the primary means of countering such attempts.

While aiming at a comprehensive and balanced presentation, I make an argument here. In its broadest outline, that argument is that utopianism is essential for the improvement of the human condition, and in this sense opponents of utopianism are both wrong and potentially dangerous. But I also argue that if used wrongly, and it has been, utopianism is itself dangerous, and in this sense supporters of utopianism are both wrong and potentially dangerous. Therefore, the conclusion both explores and attempts to rectify the contradictory nature of utopianism.

Chapter 1
Good places and bad places

The two traditions: utopia before *Utopia*

> Peace, first of all, was as readily available as washing-
> water. The earth didn't produce fear or diseases. Instead,
> what they needed appeared spontaneously, because every
> torrent-gully flowed with wine, and barley-cakes fought
> with loaves of bread around people's mouths, begging them
> to gulp down the whitest ones, if they would be so kind.

> (Teleclides, *Amphictyonies*)

> They did not marry wives, but had their women in common:
> the children so born were brought up in common and
> treated with equal affection by all. While they were infants
> the women who suckled them often exchanged their charges,
> so that even the mothers could not recognise their own
> children: consequently there was no jealousy among them,
> and they always lived without any quarrels, counting concord
> the chief of all blessings.

> (Iambulus, *Heliopolis*)

While the word 'utopia' was coined by Thomas More in 1516 and a
genre of literature developed from his book, the idea of utopia is
much older. The two quotations above and Illustrations 2 and 3
reflect two very different versions of the good life. One focuses on

2. The frontispiece to the 1518 edition of Thomas More's *Utopia* is a woodcut by Ambrosius Holbien (c. 1494–c. 1519) and depicts the country of Utopia

3. Pieter Breughel the Elder's (c. 1525–69) painting of the *Land of Cockaigne* (1567) depicts the excess of drink and food that would be possible in Cockaigne, a land of plenty that many tales say can only be reached by the poor

pleasure, and bodily pleasure in particular, with plenty of food and drink at its centre, with, in some versions, lots of readily available sex. The other focuses on social organization. The first is fantasy and is brought into being by Nature, God, or the gods; the second is presented realistically and is brought about by human beings using their intelligence. Both versions are ancient and both continue today. For some, only the second qualifies as a utopia, but others see the first as an important current in the river that is utopia.

The first has been called 'the utopia of escape' and 'the body utopia', and there is no culture without such utopias. In the traditions that make up its history in the West, it is found in the biblical Eden, Greek and Roman stories of the earthly paradise and the idea of a golden race or age in the past, and the Irish 'Vision of MacConglinne'. It moves into the 'world turned upside down' tradition with Saturnalia, the Feast of Fools, Cockaigne, and early versions of Carnival, all of which temporarily place the poor and oppressed in positions of power and their supposed superiors under them for a day or a week. It tends to be created anew and re-emerge in suppressed groups and in times of economic hardship.

The classic myths

While there were differences among these myths, they had much in common. Some parts were stated positively: humans and the gods were close and the earth spontaneously produced an abundance of food and whatever else people needed. But most were stated negatively and were concerned with solving the problems of the present: there was no fear of wild animals; there was no human conflict; there was no need to work; there was no commerce or government because they were not needed. Both the beginning and ending of life were easy: women gave birth without pain or there was no birth; there was no death, hence no need for birth, or an easy death. Some of them also explained how we got from the good life to the hardships of the present. For example, disobedience to God in Eden led to fear, toil, death, and pain in giving birth.

The most influential of these early myths are creation myths like the golden age and earthly paradise and myths of the afterlife like the Islands of the Blest, where heroes go after death, and Hades. Such myths from ancient Greece and Rome, Sumer, and early Judaism were central to the development of Western utopianism, and similar myths, such as the Chinese 'Peach Blossom Spring', are found in most early civilizations. The classic Western statement of the golden age is that of the Greek poet Hesiod (late 8th century BCE), who wrote:

> Golden was the race of speech-endowed human beings which the immortals, who have their mansions on Olympus, made first of all. They lived at the time of Cronus, when he was king in the sky; just like gods they spent their lives, with a spirit free from care, entirely apart from toil and distress. Worthless old age did not oppress them, but they were always the same in feet and hands, and delighted in festivities, lacking in all evils; and they died as if overpowered by sleep. They had all good things: the

grain-giving field bore crops of its own accord, much and
unstinting, and they themselves, willing, mild-mannered, shared
out the fruits of the labour together with many good things,
wealthy in sheep, dear to the blessed gods.

But the version of the golden age that passed down into the Middle
Ages was that of the Roman author Ovid (43 BCE to 17/18 CE).
While Hesiod stressed abundance shared equally, a joyful life, and
an easy death, Ovid, responding to current issues, added freedom
from law courts, a local community, and no war, saying:

In the beginning was the Golden Age, when men of their own accord,
without threat of punishment, without laws, maintained good faith
and did what was right. There were no penalties to be afraid of, no
bronze tablets were erected, carrying threats of legal action, no crowd
of wrong-doers, anxious for mercy, trembled before the face of their
judge: indeed, there were no judges, men lived securely without them.
Never yet had any pine tree, cut down from its home on the mountains
been launched on ocean's waves, to visit foreign lands: men knew only
their own shores. Their cities were not yet surrounded by sheer moats,
they had no straight brass trumpets, no coiling brass helmets and no
swords. The peoples of the world, untroubled by any fears, enjoyed a
leisurely and peaceful existence, and had no use for soldiers.

The changes Ovid made show how these stories reflected current
issues even as they appear to be out of time altogether.

The quotation from Teleclides at the beginning of this chapter is
another example of life in the age of Cronus, and the Roman poet
Lucian of Samosato (c. 125 to after 180) has Cronus say:

during my week the serious is barred; no business allowed.
Drinking and being drunk, noise and games and dice, appointing
of kings and feasting of slaves, singing naked, clapping of
tremulous hands, an occasional ducking of corked faces in icy
water, – such are the functions over which I preside.

The Roman festival of Saturn, known as the Saturnalia, was an actual festival in which the golden age was to return briefly, where masters waited on servants and the rich fed the poor and, in some versions, forgave debts. For all, there was gluttony and a degree of sexual freedom. And, without the gluttony and sexual freedom, the idea of a period in which debts are forgiven, thus giving the debtor a fresh start, is enshrined in the Old Testament, 'every creditor shall release what he has lent to his neighbor; he shall not exact it to his neighbor, his brother, because the Lord's release has been proclaimed' (Deuteronomy 15:2).

In the Middle Ages, descendants of Saturnalia, such as Carnival, when the poor ruled for a time, and the Feast of Fools, in which the Church hierarchy was briefly reversed and which was particularly popular in France, caused serious problems. From time to time, Carnival got out of hand, at least from the point of view of those in power, because the powerless thought that the reversal should last longer than a few days. And the Feast of Fools was vigorously suppressed by the Church. Carnival still exists in some places such as New Orleans and Rio de Janeiro, but it is no longer considered a threat.

In the Middle Ages, the Greek and Roman gods were dropped and a similar story known as the Cockaigne, or Cokaygne, which has been called 'the poor man's paradise', developed in a number of European countries. One medieval version of the Cockaigne says:

> There are rivers broad and fine
> Of oil, milk, honey and of wine;
> Water serveth there no thing
> But for sight and for washing.
> Many fruits grow in that place
> For all delight and sweet solace.

This imagery occurs again and again under different names throughout history. When everything seems hopeless, fantasy can be particularly powerful.

The Roman writer Virgil (70–19 BCE) made significant changes to the myths. First, and most importantly, in his famous Fourth Eclogue, also known as the messianic Eclogue, he moved the past golden age to the future. Second, the better world became based on human activity rather than simply being a gift from the gods: people work, primarily in agriculture, and this continues as the myth of the happy peasant or farmer, a more realistic – if still idealized – vision. This myth has never died and exists today as a substantial part of modern utopianism.

Virgil's images of the simple life in Arcadia are something of a transition between the fantasy of the first tradition and the human-created utopia of the second. And it is the human-created societies depicted by Greek and Roman writers that are most similar to More's *Utopia* and the works that followed it. This branch of the utopian tradition gives people hope because it is more realistic and because it focuses on humans solving human problems, such as adequate food, housing, and clothing and security, rather than relying on Nature or the gods.

In the West, the formal utopia appears to have originated in classical Greece, with descriptions of the Greek city-state Sparta being the most influential. The Greek writer Plutarch (46–120 CE) described the motivation of Lycurgus, the supposed founder of Sparta, and the description could well fit others, saying,

> He was convinced that a partial change of the laws would be of no avail whatsoever, but that he must proceed as a physician would with a patient who was debilitated and full of all sorts of diseases; he must reduce and alter the existing temperament by means of drugs and purges, and introduce a new and different regimen.

The society Lycurgus may have instituted at Sparta was based on the most rigorous equality among citizens, but only among citizens (there were slaves, and women were not citizens). Sparta was a military regime, and in Lycurgus's Sparta every person was to completely dedicate themselves to the country. They were to lose themselves in the whole; 'he trained his fellow-citizens to have neither the wish nor the ability to live for themselves'.

Many commentators connect Sparta with the *Republic*, the best-known utopia of the Greek philosopher Plato (428/27–348/47 BCE), which is treated as the fount of Western utopianism. The *Republic* is primarily concerned with developing an understanding of justice. It is a typical Platonic dialogue of the early to middle period in which a question is set by Socrates (469–399 BCE) and a process of question and answer takes place until a number of positions have been presented, all of which are rejected by Socrates. He then provides his own answer, gradually dominating the discussion, turning it into a monologue with only the most perfunctory interjections from the others.

The society Plato describes in the *Republic* is the closest possible approximation to the ideal society. It has three classes, corresponding to the three fundamental elements of the soul or psyche. These classes are the philosopher-kings (or reason), the auxiliaries (or the spirited element), and the artisans (who represent temperance or moderation). Most of the *Republic* is concerned with the first two classes, known collectively as the guardians, and Plato tells us little about the vast majority of the population, except to imply that in this well-regulated city-state, or *polis*, each individual will be fitted into the vocation that best suits him or her. As a result, everyone will be happy.

However, any society created by humans can only be a poor reflection of the ideal, and it must fail. Plato explores the process of failure at considerable length; in doing so, he develops a theory of corruption and applies it to both individuals and societies. The important thing here is not the theory but the underlying point that there cannot be a perfect society or human being on this earth. The best we can achieve is an approximation, which will inevitably collapse.

While the essential ingredients (harmony, knowledge, the good life of the good person) of the *Laws*, Plato's other major utopia, are identical to those of the *Republic*, the way these are achieved is different. There is the obvious difference that the *polis* of the *Laws* is based on law whereas the *polis* of the *Republic* is based on human wisdom as personified in philosopher-kings. It seems that Plato, despairing of finding or creating the conditions for developing philosopher-kings, was determined to provide the next best thing: the law code philosopher-kings would lay down for a *polis* unable to reach the level of the *polis* of the *Republic*. He even provided a substitute for the philosopher-kings in a nocturnal council which could overturn the laws if it chose.

Greek utopians, including Plato, had as a basic assumption what we call the small or face-to-face community. It was inconceivable to them that a good society could be a large one in which citizens could not all regularly meet and converse. The idea that something bigger might be possible surfaced only as Greece declined and Rome grew.

The first great anti-utopian, the Greek writer of comedies Aristophanes (448–380 BCE), wrote at the same time and discussed many of the same themes as the utopian writers. From the utopian perspective, the most important of his plays was *Ecclesiazusae, or Women in Parliament*, in which a group of women succeeded in taking over the legislative assembly and enacting a form of communism. Their legislation failed not because it was bad but because the human race was not capable of the required altruism. This is a standard reason given for rejecting utopias. A similar point was made by Aristophanes in *Plutus*, in which the blind god of wealth is given sight, whereupon he redistributes wealth to the deserving, and then human greed rapidly redistributes it again inequitably.

Since the Greek philosopher Aristotle (384–322 BCE) rejected Plato's utopia and poured scorn on the other ideal states which he discussed, he is not usually considered a utopian, but in Book VII of the *Politics*, Aristotle provided the basic characteristics of an ideal state in some detail.

Aristotle believed the best state to be one as close to self-sufficiency as possible within the limits imposed by a small population and territory, and his utopia was based on the possibility of citizens knowing each other. Also, Aristotle's utopia provided the best life for its citizens: the life of the mind, or the contemplative life, which is not a withdrawn, solitary life but the life of intellectual intercourse. Aristotle believed that this would require that there be non-citizens to do the demeaning labour, thereby freeing the citizens to lead the full life. At other places, he discussed, in more general terms, the characteristics of what might be called the best possible state.

Myths and literature after More

After More wrote *Utopia*, most of the myths gradually lost their power, but their essence continued in cockaigne-like African-American tales that are found in parallel with the spirituals that gave a foretaste of the glories of the afterlife, and songs of the 1930s depression in the United States such as 'The Sweet Potato Mountains' and 'The Big Rock Candy Mountains'.

One slave story tells of being convinced

> that in Arkansas the hogs just laying around already baked with the knives and forks sticking in them ready for to be et, and that there was fritter ponds everywhere with the fritters a-frying in them ponds of grease, and there was money trees where all you had to do was to pick the money offen 'em like picking cotton offen the stalk...

And 'The Sweet Potato Mountains' contains the refrain

Oh, cigarette vines and ham 'n' egg trees, And bread sprouts from the ground, Where white-line springs squirt booze to your knees, And there's plenty to go 'round'.

A variant of the traditional myth can be seen in the novel and film *Lost Horizon* (1933, film directed by Frank Capra 1937) loosely based on the myth of Shambhala, a Tibetan Buddhist legend of a mythical kingdom hidden somewhere in inner Asia where some of the Bodhisattvas, the most enlightened Buddhists, live. In the novel, this becomes Shangri-la, a lost community in Tibet in which people live extremely long lives.

This is not the place for a history of utopian literature, but it is necessary to say something about it and how it was used. Post-More utopias have often been characterized as focusing on the city. The historian and architectural critic Lewis Mumford (1895–1990) in particular argued that the city and the utopia were closely linked, and the following quotations from utopias from the late 19th and mid-20th centuries illustrate views of utopian architecture.

> At my feet lay a great city. Miles of broad streets, shaded by trees and lined with fine buildings, for the most part not in continuous blocks but set in larger or smaller enclosures, stretched in every direction. Every quarter contained large open squares filled with trees, among which statues glistened and fountains flashed in the late afternoon sun. Public buildings of a colossal size and an architectural grandeur unparalleled in my day raised their stately piles on every side.
>
> (Edward Bellamy, *Looking Backward*)

> She saw... a river, little no account buildings, strange structures like long-legged birds with sails that turned in the wind, a few large terracotta and yellow buildings and one blue dome, irregular buildings, none bigger than a supermarket in her day, an ordinary supermarket in any shopping plaza. The bird objects were the

tallest things around and they were scarcely higher than some of the pine trees she could see. A few lumpy free-form structures with green vines.

(Marge Piercy, *Woman on the Edge of Time*)

Contrary to much commentary, which tends to see utopia up to the middle of the 20th century as representing some form of common ownership, utopias have been written from every conceivable position. There are socialist, capitalist, monarchical, democratic, anarchist, ecological, feminist, patriarchal, egalitarian, hierarchical, racist, left-wing, right-wing, reformist, free love, nuclear family, extended family, gay, lesbian, and many more utopias, and all these types were published between 1516 and the middle of the 20th century, before diversity really took hold. And, because there is a strong anti-utopian tradition, the number could be doubled by simply putting 'anti-' in front of any of these words, and after the early 20th century there have been dystopias written reflecting all these positions.

All these different works were responding to issues that their authors thought were important to bringing about a better society. Most of the issues are perennial, such as law and order, religious belief and practice, economic relations, governance, and child-rearing and education. But the importance of the issues changes depending on the time in which the utopias were written. Utopias are reflections of the issues that were important to the period in which their authors lived.

The solutions proposed are more limited in type, if not in detail, than the issues – a reformed religion that is actually practised by believers, new laws or law codes that are enforced fairly, better economic systems, improved political systems, better education, and intelligent use of science and technology are among the most common solutions. Many utopias are nostalgic in that they look back to an idealized past which is then moved into the future, with the utopia found in living the cleaned-up version rather than the way people had actually lived. Other standard themes include a simpler life and getting a better balance between the city and country. But all of these have also been presented as being done poorly or to advantage particular individuals or groups (economic, gender, power, and so forth) and producing dystopias. For the utopian, human intelligence and ingenuity know no bounds; for the dystopian, human greed and stupidity know no bounds. And both appear to be right.

As with any genre of literature, there have been certain well-known texts or writers that appear to define the genre. While less-known texts may actually be more typical of their period, it is the best-known works that drive the literature on.

More's *Utopia*

More's *Utopia* is a complicated little book and interpreters have claimed it for radically different positions, from traditional Roman Catholicism to British imperialism to Marxism, sometimes by simply ignoring the complexity of the book and at other times making it even more complex. One set of problems stems from the fact that *Utopia* appears on the surface to be straightforward while it is quite playful and satirical. And generations of translators have misled their readers by ignoring the wordplay that would have been obvious to those reading the original Latin. There is not a lot of it, but when you discover that Anydrus, the name of the main river, means 'no water' and the surname of the person describing Utopia, Hythlodaeus, means 'speaker of nonsense', you must begin to wonder. But Raphael, Hythlodaeus's first name, means 'healer from God', so you cannot draw a clear conclusion. In a letter to Peter Giles, published in the 1517 edition of *Utopia*, More satirically commented on the play on words. Discussing a critic who could not tell whether *Utopia* was truth or fiction, More commented that if it had been fiction he would have indicated it. He wrote:

Thus, if I had done nothing else than impose names on ruler, river, city, and island such as might suggest to the more learned that the island was nowhere, the city a phantom, the river without water, and the ruler without a people, it would have been much wittier than what I actually did. Unless the faithfulness of an historian had been binding on me, I am not so stupid as to have preferred to use those barbarous and meaningless names, Utopia, Anydrus, Amaurotum, and Ademus.

But Utopia, Anydrus, Amaurotum, and Ademus do mean the island was nowhere, the city a phantom, the river without water, and the ruler without a people.

Another problem is that *Utopia* includes institutions presented positively that either were against Roman Catholic Church teachings, like voluntary euthanasia, or that More rejected later in life, like religious toleration. For some interpreters, a means must be found that excludes these institutions; St Thomas More, who died for his beliefs, must never have thought differently than his interpreters believed he should or, like his close friend the Dutch humanist and theologian Erasmus (1466/69–1536), playfully tried out ideas that he later came to reject.

In modern eyes, the society described in *Utopia* is not very attractive; it is authoritarian, hierarchical, patriarchal, and practises slavery for relatively minor offences. But through the eyes of an early 16th-century reader, these things were the norm, and slavery in Utopia was a more humane punishment than many that would have been imposed at the time, when some minor offences were punished by death. And, most importantly, no one in Utopia was poor or rich, achieved by reducing demand, everyone working, sharing equally, and living simply. Thus, to many in the 16th century, Utopia would have seemed like paradise.

Satire

The satire running throughout More's *Utopia* is fundamental to both utopian traditions because one of the functions of most utopias is to hold the present up to ridicule and, in doing so, many utopias use a typical tool of satire, exaggeration. And in some, like the English novelist Samuel Butler's (1835–1902) *Erewhon or Over the Range* (1872), it is impossible to be certain what, if any, positive position is being advocated. In *Erewhon*, for example, criminals are treated as sick and sent to doctors, but the sick are thrown in jail. A small sub-genre that can be called 'Erewhonian' has developed from this book.

More typical is the Irish satirist Jonathan Swift's (1667–1745) *Travels into Several Remote Nations of the World* (1726), now known as *Gulliver's Travels*. The fourth book of *Gulliver's Travels* is the good place in the book, but its dominant inhabitants are horses not humans. The humans, Yahoos, are animalistic and the horses, Houyhnhnms, are rational, so what is Swift saying about humans and about reason? *Gulliver's Travels* gave rise to a large sub-genre known as Gulliveriana, little of which is as subtle as the original, with much of the literature simply endowing some animal with human characteristic. Recently, much has been written about Gulliver's wife, whom he regularly abandoned.

Around the same time that Swift was writing, the English writer Daniel Defoe (1660–1731) published *The Life and Strange Surprizing Adventures of Robinson Crusoe, of York, Mariner* (1719), now known as *Robinson Crusoe*, which was based on a real incident in which a man, the Scottish sailor Alexander Selkirk (1676–1721), was shipwrecked alone on an isolated island for four years. Since Crusoe is alone and not particularly content for most of the novel, it is hard to see it as positive or negative, and that does not change when Crusoe is joined by Friday, a native of a nearby island whom Crusoe rescues from cannibals. But *Robinson Crusoe* gave rise to a large sub-genre, the Robinsonade, that is often utopian and usually includes a group of people being shipwrecked, the best known being *The Swiss Family Robinson* (1812–13) by the Swiss writer Johann David Wyss (1743–1818), which was made into a popular film.

The Bellamy effect

The great utopians of the late 19th and early 20th centuries were the American Edward Bellamy (1850–98) and the English writers William Morris (1834–96) and H. G. Wells (1866–1946). Bellamy's *Looking Backward: 2000–1887 A.D.* (1888) sold very well around the world and produced a substantial upsurge in the production of utopias that lasted until World War I. Bellamy's utopia was set in a future Boston, Massachusetts, that had evolved into a society where the antagonism between capitalism and labour had been overcome. As corporations became bigger and bigger and became monopolies controlling most of the economy, they were nationalized or simply taken over by the state, with workers becoming employees of the state. Hours of work varied based on the unpleasantness and danger of the work, and everyone retired at 45.

William Morris wrote a review of *Looking Backward* in which he deplored Bellamy's 'machine-life' with its emphasis on making work tolerable by reducing the amount of work rather than reducing 'the *pain of labour* to a minimum'. Morris then wrote *News from Nowhere; or, An Epoch of Rest* (1890) to depict a society that stressed craftsmanship and the local community. Whereas Bellamy has an elaborate political system, Morris uses the Houses of Parliament to store manure and says 'we have no longer anything which you would call politics'. Bellamy wrote a generally favourable review of *News from Nowhere*, although he said it needed more detail.

But the most prolific writer of utopias was H. G. Wells, who wrote both positive utopias and dystopias. While they vary widely, there are central themes. One is the conflict between capital and labour, what might happen if it is not solved, and how to solve it. Another is the desirability of world government.

Wells is best described as a pessimistic utopian, a man who believed that it was possible to radically improve human life but doubted that the willpower to do so would be found. He never gave up hope, but he never stopped doubting either. *The Time Machine* (1895), one of Wells's earliest and most successful novels, is set far in the future with the descendants of capital and labour still in conflict. Most of his other utopias and dystopias are set in nearer futures and some, particularly the dystopias, can be read as stages towards the future depicted in *The Time Machine*, with the division between the capital and labour becoming more and more extreme. The utopias and much of Wells's non-utopian political writings suggest ways that the negative futures can be avoided. Wells believed that intelligence, particularly scientific intelligence, applied to social problems was the answer. In *A Modern Utopia* (1905), he depicts an association of men and women, called the Samurai, who, living according to a strict code of behaviour and dedicated to service, had created and maintained the much better society Wells believed possible.

He called for the creation of such a group, which he most frequently called 'the Open Conspiracy', in many works, and he advocated many reforms, from birth control to a world encyclopedia, as small steps in the right direction. Wells was clearly frustrated that his ideas were not adopted more often, and he worked hard to sell his ideas and to improve education, particularly scientific education, in the hope that a better-educated population would be more receptive to his proposals. But Wells is best known for his non-utopian science fiction, his dystopias, and some of his comic novels, rather than for his utopias and his political writing.

The growth of the dystopia

And with World Wars I and II, the flu epidemic, the Depression, the Korean War, the war in Vietnam, and other events of the 20th century, dystopias became the dominant form of utopian literature. While the word 'dystopia' was first used in the middle of the 18th century, and the English philosopher John Stuart Mill (1806–73) used it in a speech in Parliament in 1868, the literary form and the use of the word to describe it did not become common until well into the 20th century.

In 1883, Francis Galton (1822–1911) coined the term 'eugenic' referring to the ability to produce superior offspring, with specific reference to humans rather than animals. A movement developed with the idea of improving the human stock through selective breeding for certain characteristics (positive eugenics) or selective breeding to avoid certain characteristics (negative eugenics). Many utopias were written, including two unpublished ones by Galton ('Kantsaywhere' and 'The Donoghues of Dunno Weir'), reflecting this movement. Many of the utopias, including Galton's, believing that selective breeding alone would not be enough to produce the desired result, were as concerned with the social conditions into which children were born and how they were raised as they were with the physical and moral characteristics of the parents. Other works were primarily concerned with selective breeding, focusing on the elimination of undesirable characteristics by prohibiting people who exhibited them from having children or by requiring people with the desired characteristics to have children with each other. Both approaches produced dystopias, either by virtue of disagreements over the traits chosen or worries about the potential for misuse of the power to make the choices.

Proposals to select on racial and ethnic grounds were common and, where the power to do so existed, put into practice. The best-known programme was that of Germany under the National Socialists, when people with characteristics designated for elimination were not merely prevented from having children but were killed. Less well known, Germany also practised positive eugenics, breeding people with desired traits. Utopias were published in Germany and other countries depicting the better society to be produced by such programmes.

There were a number of Nazi utopias published, such as Ernst Bergmann's *Deutschland, das Bildungsland der neuen Menschen* (*Germany, the Cultural Land of the New Man*; 1933), but there were also a large number of anti-German and anti-Nazi dystopias, with *Swastika Night* (1937) by Katherine Burdekin (1896–1963), writing as Murray Constantine, among the most powerful.

The same period that produced many anti-German and anti-Soviet dystopias also saw the publication of three outstanding works: the Russian Evgeny Zamiatin's (1884–1937) *We* (written in Russian in 1920, but first published in English in 1924), and the English writers Aldous Huxley's (1894–1963) *Brave New World* (1932) and George Orwell's (born Eric Blair, 1903–50) *Nineteen Eighty-Four* (1949; Orwell insisted that the title be spelled out). While all three target the misuse of power, each is a many-faceted, complex work with multiple concerns, and they all attack capitalism as much as they attack communism. All three depict partially failed attempts to control the power of sexual desire. *We* licenses sexual behaviour in a way that is meant to meet individual needs; *Brave New World* insists on promiscuity; and *Nineteen Eighty-Four* severely restricts sex. And all three imply that this may be an area that even a totalitarian regime would not be able to control.

Huxley wrote in *Brave New World Revisited* (1958) that he had simply projected into the future things that he had observed at the time of writing and that had worried him, and that 25 years later, the future of *Brave New World* seemed to be coming much faster than he had expected in the 1930s. He had also written that if he were to rewrite *Brave New World*, he would have provided a more positive alternative, and he did just that in his utopia *Island* (1962), which depicts a good society in which promiscuity is transformed into free love, with the emphasis on love; the drug Soma, used in *Brave New World* to escape from problems, is replaced with Moksha Medicine (akin to peyote or LSD), which leads to enlightenment; and the other negatives of *Brave New World* become positives, at least partially through the power of religion. But at the end, the utopia is crushed by the outside world because it has oil.

Huxley's projection or extrapolation into the future of trends he saw around him became the norm for dystopias. While dystopias tend to differ from utopias in not being described by an outside visitor but from within, they are clearly connected to the present in which they are written. In that connection, they provide an explicitly positive message to go with the negative one. They say, as H. G. Wells constantly said, that this is what will happen if we fail to act, but if we do act, this future can still be avoided. Most writers of dystopias left it at that, as a warning, but Wells put much effort into spelling out just what he thought needed to be done and how to do it.

While the dystopia became the dominant literary form of the 20th century, the utopia was not displaced, and at the same time that the great dystopias of the first half of the 20th century were being published, there were many utopias published, and utopian movements flourished particularly during the 1930s depression. In the USA, the novelist Upton Sinclair (1878–1968) combined the two, writing a number of utopias such as *We, People of America and How We Ended Poverty* (1935) and running to be governor of California with a programme called EPIC, or End Poverty in California. Also, the technocracy movement that proposed replacing politicians with engineers and scientists produced a number of utopias, notably *Life in a Technocracy* (1933) by Harold Loeb (1891–1974). Other similar movements emerged in most countries faced with the economic and social problems of the time. But as the possibility of war became of greater and greater concern, the dystopia dominated the scene until after World War II.

In Britain, both during the war and in the immediate aftermath, works such as J. B. Priestley's (1894–1984) 'They Came to a City' (1944) and C. E. M. Joad's (1891–1953) *The Adventures of the Young Soldier in Search of the Better World* (1943) speculated about the better society that could be created after victory was achieved. After the Labour Party won the 1945 election, books like James Hanley's (1901–85) *What Farrar Saw* (1946) and Somerset De Chair's (1911–95) *The Teetotalitarian State* (1947) satirized Labour Party policy.

The 'Sixties'

While utopias were published throughout the period that the dystopia dominated, they went unnoticed until the upsurge in utopianism in the so-called 'Sixties' (the actual dates varied from country to country). Much of the utopian impulse in this period led to the streets, to, for example, the 1968 uprising in Czechoslovakia, the 1968 rebellion in Paris with its explicitly utopian message '*Le réalisme qui demande l'impossible*' ('Be realistic, demand the impossible'), and the civil rights movement in the United States. In addition, many intentional communities, then universally known as communes, were founded, many of which still exist over 40 years later. And utopian literature flourished, but it was a literature with a difference, a chastened literature that knew that achieving a better society would not be easy. Its societies were populated with men and women with real human strengths and weaknesses, and even the much better societies still have problems, even serious ones. Ursula K. Le Guin's (b. 1929) *The Dispossessed* (1974) had the subtitle *An Ambiguous Utopia*, and that subtitle fits many of the other works published at the time. The literary scholar Tom Moylan (b. 1943) called these works 'critical utopias', the political theorist Lucy Sargisson (b. 1964), focusing on feminist utopianism, called them 'transgressive utopias', and I have called some of them 'flawed utopias' to illustrate the way in which some authors, like Ursula K. Le Guin in her 'The Ones Who Walk Away From Omelas' (1973), present what appears to be a utopia but may in fact be a dystopia.

The feminist utopia was the most important of the streams coming out of Sixties utopianism and produced most of the novels of the period that are still read. In 1972, Joanna Russ (b. 1937) published an essay entitled 'What Can a Heroine Do? Or Why Women Can't Write', arguing that contemporary societies were so sexist that only by inventing new worlds was it possible for women to create fully rounded female characters. And feminist utopianism was a significant part of the feminist movement. The best-known feminist utopias were Russ's *The Female Man* (1975), Marge Piercy's (b. 1936) *Woman on the Edge of Time* (1976), and a number of short stories by Alice Bradley Sheldon (1915–87), writing as James Tiptree, Jr, such as 'Houston Houston, Do You Read?' (1976).

Utopia today

Aspects of the utopianism of the Sixties were part of long-term changes in Western societies, but there was a backlash against these changes, and, while utopias continued to be published, utopian literature mostly returned to the dystopia. Except for lesbian utopias, feminist utopias almost disappeared in the 1990s, although there has been a resurgence since 2000. The great exception to the return to the dystopia has been in the environmental utopia. Certainly, many dystopias have depicted the horrors of a future environmental collapse, but Kim Stanley Robinson (b. 1952) and others have published important environmental utopias. Robinson has published two trilogies with environmental themes, the Mars trilogy (1992, 1993, 1996) and a climate change/global warming trilogy whose first volume, *Forty Signs of Rain* (2004), depicts the dystopia brought about by the failure of politicians to deal with global warming and the two other volumes, *Fifty Degrees Below* (2005) and *Sixty Days and Counting* (2007), deal with a change in policy and its ultimately positive results. And the whole subgenre of the ecotopia, named after Ernest Callenbach's (b. 1928) 1975 novel of that name is today the strongest utopian current, and many ecotopias are also feminist, so that the two strongest currents of the last 50 years are now often combined. For example, novels by Sally Miller Gearhart (b. 1931) such as

The Wanderground: Stories of the Hill Women (1978) and *The Magister* (2003) combine both feminist and ecological perspectives.

Utopian literature is constantly changing, adding new forms. Today, most is complex or ambiguous, presenting better but flawed societies, or worse societies with something still good about them. A recent change is the migration of utopias to the internet and publish-on-demand publishers (it regularly appeared in pod's previous incarnation, 'vanity' presses). Works posted on the web and pod publications are more likely to read like some of the older utopias, with simple, one-size-fits-all answers to complex questions, but some, like Merritt Abrash's (b. 1930) *Mindful of Utopia* (2002), are as complex as other contemporary works. Such forms of publication have added to the contemporary growth of utopian literature, but, as with many past utopias, much of it goes unread, to the frustration of its authors.

Chapter 2
Utopian practice

Over the centuries, many individuals and groups have attempted to put their visions into practice. Some tried to gain political power to do so (few succeeded) and others created social movements (with greater success). Those utopians who gained political power often created dystopias rather than utopias, with, in the 20th century, countries like Nazi Germany under Adolf Hitler (1889–1945) and Cambodia/Kampuchea under Pol Pot (1928–98) being noteworthy examples.

But the most common form of putting a specific vision into practice has been to create a small community either to withdraw from the larger society to practise the beliefs of its members without interference or to demonstrate to the larger society that their utopia could be put into practice. Although he denied the utopian connection, the historian Arthur Eugene Bestor, Jr (1908–94) called the latter 'patent-office models of the good society', a label that actually makes the utopian connection.

In addition, small, temporary actions are now being seen as utopian because they generally employ a utopian image against the dystopia that, as their proponents see it, they oppose. These actions take place in many different ways, from performance to protest.

Intentional communities

What we now most often call intentional communities, popularly known as communes, have had many names in the past, a number of which relate directly to utopianism, such as utopian community, utopian experiment, practical utopia, alternative society, and experimental community. These labels and their variants have either never been accepted or have since been dropped in favour of a more neutral term; many people living in such communities have rejected the label 'utopian' and prefer 'intentional community'. Still, even given this rejection and the fact that most such communities have not been utopian in the ways the word is commonly used, there are close connections between utopianism and such communities.

There is no absolutely agreed upon definition of an intentional community, but many would agree with something like mine:

> A group of five or more adults and their children, if any, who come from more than one nuclear family and who have chosen to live together to enhance their shared values or for some other mutually agreed upon purpose.

The most important part of this definition and the part that connects such communities with utopianism is the emphasis on living a life based on 'shared values' or a 'mutually agreed upon purpose'.

All communities, even those who believe that they are waiting for the Second Coming of Christ in the near future, have constitutions, rules and regulations, and/or agreements (formal or informal) about how their members are to live their lives. If these documents and agreements had been fictions, we would call them utopias without question, and often they are fictions in the sense that they do not accurately reflect how the community actually functions.

Intentional communities have been established so that their members can live a particular way of life. Some have sought to change sexual behavior radically. Many have changed how people ate, and the vegetarian communities changed what people ate. Many communities have changed how work was organized, and particularly have broken down gender distinctions in how work was to be allocated. Others worked with some success at breaking down the distinction between mental and physical labour.

Many have been religious and they tried to lead a way of life that their members believed their faith required. Many have followed a charismatic leader, preaching their version of religious belief, gaining followers, and establishing communities. Others have followed the ideas of a social theorist. There are many other reasons that people choose to withdraw from mainstream society to live differently.

The first such religious communities were probably Hindu ashrams and then Buddhist monasteries. Among the first such groups to withdraw to practise their beliefs in what became part of the Western traditions were the Essenes, a Jewish religious group that existed in many cities from the 2nd century BCE to the 1st century CE, established the Qumran community, and produced the Dead Sea Scrolls, thought to have been their library. Most Essenes were celibate, and they lived communally. Later, some of the earliest specifically Christian communities formed around individual holy men, usually hermits, known collectively as the Desert Fathers.

Many of the religious withdrawn communities based their practices on their interpretation of the early church in Jerusalem, particularly the description of community of goods found in Acts 2:44–45 – 'And all who believed were together and had all things in common; and they sold their possessions and goods and distributed them to all, as any had need' – which was constantly referred to in the descriptions of themselves by later communities.

And many of the founders of the communities believed that the communal practices of the early church reflected the intention of Jesus. Later, community property was thought to be appropriate for those who dedicated themselves to the Church but not for laypeople.

Christian convents and monasteries

The first major step in the creation of the Christian monastic tradition was *The Rule of St Benedict*, in which Benedict (480?–?543) gave details of an order designed to provide a structured setting within which it would be possible to lead a better life, closer to the ideal Christian life. Benedict's Rule requires that no monk have any property, saying, 'more than anything else is this vice of property to be cut off root and branch from the monastery'. Details are given on the amount of food to be given out (Rule XXXIX) and the amount of wine to be allowed – one pint per day (Rule XL). A rule specifies the amount of manual work and opposes idleness (Rule XLVIII), details the clothing to be issued (Rule LV), and, of course, the various officers, religious rituals, and procedures for admission to the monastery. These rules helped create communities designed to make the righteous life possible. Defenders of monasticism explicitly contended that most people were not capable of such a life and that only within the monastic setting would this clearly utopian goal be possible.

As monasteries prospered and monks appeared to lose the austerity originally recommended, reforms were instituted by the French St Odo of Cluny (c. 878–942), who established the Cluniac form of monastery in order to correct what he saw as the excesses of other monastic orders. St Francis of Assisi (1181/82–1226) also stressed the need for reform and proposed a wandering order of friars who were actually to practise poverty. Francis's approach was subverted by conservatives within the Church and a more traditional Franciscan order was ultimately founded.

The attempt to re-achieve the ideals of Benedict, Odo, Francis, and others is a recurring theme in the history of monasticism. A new rule is written, instituted, and practised. The monasteries become successful and fall upon good times, which are their undoing. The monks become idle and used to the good life. Then a new rule is instituted and the cycle resumes.

The Reformation produced many groups that hoped to create a life based on their reading of the New Testament. For example, the Hutterian Brethren were first established during the Radical Reformation in the 16th century. The Hutterites, as they are also known, were named after their early leader Jakob Hutter (c. 1500–36), who insisted on a community of goods and pacifism.

4. Monastic communities are among the oldest intentional communities and continue to thrive and adjust to changes in the societies in which they exist, including in their architecture, as shown by this priory of the Benedictine community in St Louis, Missouri

To escape persecution, they moved to various countries in Europe before becoming established in North America in the late 19th century. In the USA during World War I, they were prosecuted for their pacifism, and many communities moved to Canada. Today, there are almost 500 Hutterite communities, the majority of them in Canada.

Few other communities from the Reformation period still exist, but many that emerged on the Continent during the following 200 years established communities in the United States, notably the Community of True Inspiration, better known as the Amana Communities, in Iowa, which traced its origins to Germany in 1714 and the teachings of Eberhard Ludwig Gruber (d. 1728) and Johann Friedrich Rock (1678? –1749), who believed that they continued to receive direct messages from God.

Other religious groups developed in Britain and the United States and chose to establish communities to enable them to practise their beliefs. The best known are groups such as the Shakers (officially the United Society of Believers in Christ's Second Appearing) and the Oneida community. One practising Shaker community remains in Maine, but today the Shakers are best known for their craftsmanship. The Oneida community did not last as long and became a stock company producing Oneida Silverplate. But at their height, both were known for their characteristic sexual practices, the Shakers being celibate and the Oneida community practising what they called 'complex marriage', with all community members assumed to be married to all others, although sexual relations were not generally promiscuous. Both believed in and tried to practise gender equality, with the Shakers believing that the Second Coming of Christ had occurred in the female form in their founder Ann Lee (1736–84). And the Oneida community instituted a eugenic experiment by choosing those who were allowed to have children together. The experiment is generally considered successful in the sense that most of the children produced proved both healthy and intelligent, and mostly their descendants have continued to be so.

5. The Shaker meeting house at the Canterbury, New Hampshire, community showing the separate doors for men and women

Other communities were established based on the ideas of reformers, such as the men identified by Friedrich Engels (1820–95) as *utopian* socialists to distinguish them from Marxian *scientific* socialism. Engels identified three theorists as utopian socialists: the Welshman Robert Owen (1771–1858), and the Frenchmen Charles Fourier (1772–1837) and Henri Saint-Simon (1760–1825). Although none of them wrote a utopian novel, they did publish expositions of their ideal societies, and others wrote utopian novels based on the ideas of Owen and Fourier. Owen established intentional communities in the UK and the USA, and others founded communities based on his ideas in those countries and in Ireland. Owen was concerned with factory reform, and his reforms at his cotton mill in New Lanark, Scotland, were very successful. New Lanark is now a UNESCO World Heritage Site. Communities based on the proposals of Fourier and Saint-Simon were founded in France and later in the USA.

6. New Lanark was the site of Robert Owen's (1771–1858) first major step in his career as a reformer. When Owen became manager of the cotton mill at New Lanark, he provided the villagers with decent housing, education, health care, and food at affordable prices, none of which was available in most factory towns. He also abolished physical punishment and limited child labour. Owen's experiment was a great success both in the sense that productivity increased and in the sense that his workers were happier. New Lanark is now a UNESCO World Heritage Site

The kibbutz

Many religious and secular communities were established throughout the 19th and early 20th centuries, but the next major event in the history of intentional communities was the founding of Degania, the first kibbutz, in Palestine in 1920. Many Jews, most of them young people, moved to the area to establish kibbutz throughout what is now Israel. The earliest ones were mainly secular, although religious communities, called Moshav, were also established.

The kibbutz were generally successful until the combination of globalization and troubles in the Israeli economy forced many to make significant changes in their internal economies. Most kibbutz have survived their difficult times, but many are not as communal or as well-off as they once were.

Henry Near, the historian of the kibbutz movement, calls the kibbutz today 'post-utopian', arguing that the founding was clearly utopian in that it expected the kibbutzim would create wholly new and better lives for their members but that since no people or social form could ever live up to the hopes of the founding, people must adjust to the reality of daily life with other people and the loss of the original vision. It is 'post-utopian' in that many members adjust their utopian vision to the reality, some simply changing the dream, some putting it in the past, some concluding that the current situation is still better than the alternatives, and others putting utopia off to some undefined future.

At its peak, the kibbutz movement attracted a great deal of moral and financial support from the government of Israel, and a few other countries saw the advantages in supporting communal settlements. In the USA, during the depression of the 1930s about 100 communities were constructed as a means of relief and resettlement. And in New Zealand in the 1970s, a programme was put in place to establish communities known as 'Ohu', a Maori word meaning to achieve something 'by means of friendly help and work'. A few communities were established but were quickly undermined by the bureaucracy.

Dystopian communities

The Chinese communes established under Mao Zedong (1893–1976) were an authoritarian version of communalism and show that it can be dystopian in that the lives of many of the people required to join were clearly worse than they had been before. The mass suicides at Jonestown and the Solar Temple also indicate that participating in a community with an exceptionally strong, charismatic leader can lead people to do things that they probably would not do otherwise, including killing themselves. While many charges against intentional communities have been shown to be false, there are enough examples of mistreatment to require recognition of the dystopian side of communalism.

The 'Sixties' communities

The Sixties produced an explosion of intentional communities throughout the world, with thousands of mostly short-lived urban groups self-identifying as communes and hundreds of rural communities founded with varying utopian visions. Such communities were established throughout Europe and North America. Because of its perception that the communities practised free love or were promiscuous (some were, some were not), the press was fascinated by Hippie communes like the rural Drop City and the Hog Farm and Kerista in the Haight Ashbury district of San Francisco. Some urban communes served as 'safe houses' for anti-war activists trying to avoid arrest, and this led the press to condemn all communities as harbouring dangerous radicals. In both Europe and North America, the majority of communities were simply trying to practise what their members saw as a better, less materialistic, freer way of life, and the continued existence of a substantial number of them more than 40 years later suggests that some people found what they were looking for.

7. **Drop City was an intentional community established in southern Colorado in the mid-1960s. Originally established by art students from the universities of Colorado and Kansas, it became an icon of Hippie communalism. It was noted for its dome architecture**

Also, in the Sixties many people were attracted to Eastern religions, particularly Buddhism and Hinduism. As a result, Buddhist monks began to move to Western countries to teach and establish monasteries, and Hindu teachers and gurus also came to Europe and North America and established ashrams.

But the communities that were most similar to earlier communities were not based on Eastern religions but on a new vision, like the communities inspired by the behavioural psychologist B. F. Skinner's utopian novel *Walden Two*. The best known of these communities, Twin Oaks in Virginia, long ago moved away from the Skinnerian model, but the other survivor of the original Skinnerian communities, Los Horcones in Mexico, still follows aspects of the original vision of using the institutions of the community to modify and improve behaviour.

Twin Oaks is a member of the Federation of Egalitarian Communities, a small group of communities that try to meet seven criteria. These criteria are goals, aspirational rather than currently achieved, but they clearly enunciate a utopian vision. Each of the Federation communities:

1. Holds its land, labor, income and other resources in common.
2. Assumes responsibility for the needs of its members, receiving the products of their labor and distributing these and all other goods equally according to need.
3. Practices non-violence.
4. Uses a form of decision making in which members have an equal opportunity to participate, either through consensus, direct vote, or right of appeal or overrule.
5. Actively works to establish the equality of all people and does not permit discrimination on the basis of race, class, creed, ethnic origin, age, sex, sexual orientation, or gender identity.
6. Acts to conserve natural resources for present and future generations while striving to continually improve ecological awareness and practice.
7. Creates processes for group communication and participation and provides an environment which supports people's development.

And there is a network of communities in the USA centred on the magazine *Communities: Life in Cooperative Culture*, which has been published since 1972; a network in the UK centred on the series *Diggers and Dreamers*, which has been published since the early 1990s; and a worldwide network of eco-villages.

Contemporary intentional communities

Two recent movements are either directly connected with or related to communalism. The eco-village movement is clearly part of communalism, with small communities throughout the world trying to achieve a more ecologically balanced lifestyle, architecture, and community design. Some of these communities, like the Farm in Tennessee in the USA, also provide support for the development of other such communities. Some communities or individual members of communities use the expertise gained in needing to achieve consensus to train people both in other communities and outside communalism in group dynamics.

The co-housing movement, which originated in Denmark and has spread throughout Western countries, has links to intentional communities. In co-housing, property is a mixture of private and collective, with the site and shared facilities held collectively, usually as shareholders, and the individual houses owned individually. The ethos stresses community interaction. Some co-housing groups see themselves as intentional communities, but others reject the connection, and this division accurately reflects the reality of co-housing. The form of property-holding tends to be the same or at least similar, but the extent of community life varies considerably. At one end of the spectrum, community meetings, community work, shared meals, and the like are the norm. At the other end, community interaction is minimal and exists only to the extent required by the legal agreements. Most groups are somewhere in between these extremes.

Housing cooperatives, which range from a single house providing accommodation for students at a university to massive complexes, are also intentional communities. Even though the larger ones may have little communal activity, the smaller ones often physically look like an urban intentional community and function in much the same way. In addition, some producer cooperatives, such as Mondragón in Spain, are regularly included as intentional communities in that they provide not just jobs for their workers, but involve them in running the business and provide them with amenities, often including housing, that go well beyond those provided by most businesses.

It should be clear that there is no one model of community life; that intentional communities serve many purposes. For example,

Black Mountain College was a community that acted as a cultural and political centre, with the folk singer Pete Seeger (b. 1918), the composer John Cage (1912–92), and the dancer and choreographer Merce Cunningham (1919–2009) as members.

For many years, Belgium has had communities designed for the mentally ill, and such therapeutic communities have become common. In the USA, the Gould Farm community in Massachusetts and the CooperRiis community in North Carolina have long provided such a setting. The Camphill communities throughout the world, which are based on the teachings of the Austrian educator Rudolf Steiner (1861–1925), work with people who have learning disabilities, mental health problems, and other special needs, providing a secure, supportive environment in which they are able to develop as fully as possible as individuals.

A group of communities that are a variant of therapeutic communities are the Catholic Worker communities, which were established to assist alcoholics, drug addicts, and others at the very bottom of the social ladder to better themselves. Such communities include Catholic Worker houses in the worst parts of major cities and a number of rural communities where people can go for fresh air and physical labour to help their recovery. An earlier and quite similar version were the communities founded by the Salvation Army in the late 19th and early 20th centuries. City colonies and rural colonies were both established, and the plan was to expand to overseas colonies where those who had been successful in the rural communities would be able to start an entirely new life.

Successes or failures?

What makes a community a success or a failure? A standard answer is longevity, with 25 years the standard measure proposed by Rosabeth Moss Kanter (b. 1943), the Ernest L. Arbuckle Professor at Harvard Business School, in her book *Commitment and Community* (1972), but for most community members this is a deeply flawed measure. While there are many communities today that are well past the 25-year rule, including quite a few founded in the Sixties and generally thought to be long gone, for many people longevity simply misses the point.

The fact that the community lasted does not mean that it contained the same people. Some did, some did not, but most communities had significant turnover. Kanter's assumptions do appear to fit religious communities, some of which lasted for generations. If God or God's representative tells you to stay, you stay. While longevity can be a measure of success when combined with other factors, alone it is meaningless. And while Kanter herself was aware of this, the simple measure has nevertheless been applied by others since then.

One approach to success and failure is that stated by the American progressive thinker Henry Demarest Lloyd (1847–1903):

> Always failures? Only within these communities has there been
> seen, in the wide boundaries of the United States, a social life where
> hunger and cold, prostitution, intemperance, poverty, slavery, crime,
> premature old age and unnecessary mortality, panic and industrial
> terror, have been abolished. If they had done this for only a year,
> they would have deserved to be called the only successful 'society' on
> this continent, and some of them are generations old. All this has not
> been done by saints in heaven, but on earth by average men and
> women.

Another measure, and one in favour with community members, is that a community is a success to the extent that it meets the needs of its members for however long they are members. For most members, the success of the community is not the longevity of a community but rather the extent to which it did or did not improve their lives for the time they were members. Of course, needs obviously vary from member to member, and needs change as people change, so the internal dynamics of a community will change over time.

Recent developments in utopian practice

Two recent utopian practices, one of which is related to intentional communities, illustrate the way in which utopianism has moved away from the traditional categories. The first, which Hakim Bey (Peter Lamborn Wilson, b. 1945) has called TAZ, or Temporary Autonomous Zone, and George McKay (b. 1960) has called DiY (Do it Yourself) Culture, is a space of activity created for a specific purpose. Both Bey and McKay are primarily concerned with protests, but the annual lesbian music camp in Michigan and other temporary sites can be included. In retrospect, they can be called utopian because they temporarily produced what the participants saw as a better life, however briefly, and they relate back to earlier temporary utopias like Saturnalia, Carnival, the Feast of Fools, the tent meetings of some religious revivals, and the 'happenings' of the Sixties. And some create quite long-lasting communities, such as the women's peace camp at Greenham Common air base in Berkshire, England, that lasted from September 1981 until 2000.

Utopian language is also being used for even more temporary phenomena. There is, for example, the British art collective Freee (3 es) which creates political protest in public space by, among other things, simply going to a place, usually with a slogan of some sort, and standing there for hours creating a TAZ or temporary utopian space around themselves. The art is created by the people who interact with them. There are many such groups, but Freee sees what it is doing as utopian.

An aspect of this phenomenon is performance. In every performance, be it music, dance, theatre, or some forms of public art, there are at least two things going on, one among the performers and one in the audience. In rare cases, the two bond together and a truly utopian moment is created; but more often, there are what might be thought of as smaller utopian moments. More often, but still rarely, the performers create the utopian space among themselves in that one performance, and performance theorists have made the utopia connection. For example, Jill Dolan (b. 1957), a professor of drama at the University of Texas, wrote:

> I believe that theatre and performance can articulate a common future, one that's more just and equitable, one in which we can all participate more equally, with more chances to live fully and contribute to the making of culture.

There are lots of such moments, and while we know that the next performance may not reach the heights of the last one, knowing that it is possible and the feelings it produces when it happens are what is important. And it is important in ways that are potentially political because the satisfaction of that moment can leak out of the performance space to inform the dissatisfaction of everyday life.

Dissatisfaction is the beginning of utopianism, and ultimately utopianism is about the transformation of everyday life; utopianism confronts the fact that lives are wholes, that children, families, marriage, education, economics, politics, death, and so on are all connected. And intentional communities are particularly radical in that their members are willing to experiment with the transformation of their own lives. And all members of intentional communities must deal with this transformation every day.

Chapter 3
Indigenous, colonial, and postcolonial utopianism

There have been two types of colonies, and both were designed to serve the interests of the home country, not the interests of the colony. One was primarily intended to exploit the labour, raw materials, and wealth of the colony. The second was designed for settlement, either to offload surplus population or as places to send undesirables. Colonies are important to utopianism in that they represented utopian dreams themselves, but also because collectively more literary utopias have been written and more intentional communities have been established in colonies than in the countries from which they originated. All colonies had impacts on the indigenous populations, and the interpretation of those impacts have varied both over time and depending on who was doing the interpreting.

Settler colonies

The standard interpretation of the process of immigration to setter colonies is that people were both pushed from the home country by poverty, disease, and other local conditions and pulled to the new country by desire for a better life or the hope of being able to put their political or religious beliefs into practice. James Belich (b. 1956) has demonstrated in *Replenishing the Earth* (2009) that this picture is too simple. But it is also true that from the early 17th century until the mid-19th century, people left their homes and travelled, in some cases half way around the world, in the hope of being able to live in better conditions than was possible for them in their home countries. Some found a better life in the new place; others did not, and either stayed in the new country in the same or worse condition as before or returned to the home country. But the dream of a better life that drove so many was clearly utopian, and settler colonies were all informed by utopian dreams. One illustration of this can be found in the songs immigrants sang, which regularly described the place they were going to in utopian terms. For example, an Irish song, 'The Glorious and Free United States of America', makes the utopian imagery explicit:

> If you labour in America,
> In riches you will roll,
> There's neither tithes nor taxes there
> Nor rent to press you down;
> Its a glorious free country,
> To welcome every man,
> So sail off to America,
> As soon as e'er you can.

And while not part of the original intent, settler or immigrant colonies also provided a space for various dissidents, mostly religious, to try out their ideas, often in intentional communities. And utopianism has been central to the national identities of New Zealand and the United States.

Indigenous utopianism

But the dreams of the settlers clashed with the expectations of the people already living in these countries and generally produced actual dystopias for them. Such colonized peoples included the highly developed urban cultures of the Aztecs, Incas, and Mayans, and non-urban cultures like the Aborigines of Australia, the Maori of New Zealand, the First Nations and Inuit in Canada, and the Native American Indians in Canada and the United States.

All these peoples had creation myths which explained how the world and the beings populating it came about. In many of these myths, the early creation was better than what followed, and the myths included an explanation of what went wrong.

Because settler colonies often systematically destroyed the cultures of the indigenous inhabitants while also slaughtering the people, we know much less of their myths or their dreams of a good life than we do about the dreams of the settlers. But in some cases, modern, recreated, and sometimes romanticized, versions of those dreams exist, and recent research is beginning to tell us more about the myths and stories of these peoples. We are learning more because in the postcolonial period cultures that had been suppressed but had not actually disappeared are being revived and the old stories retold. As an anonymous contemporary American Indian wrote:

> To walk in the Old Ways is to live in the sacred manner, to stand upright, to walk straight, to respect our brothers and sisters of different Nations and different species. It is to open ourselves like air, like sky, in order to *know* the mountains, the waters, the wind, the lights of the sky, the plants, and the four-legged, six-legged, no-legged, and winged beings. It is to kill in the sacred manner, to know love, sorrow, anger, joy in the sacred manner, and to die in the sacred manner.

While this is a romanticized view of the past, it is clearly a statement of a utopian dream.

There are utopian traditions among the Aborigines in Australia, the First Nations in Canada, the Maori in New Zealand, and the Native American Indians in the United States. And the struggle against colonialism produced millennial movements with strong utopian elements, such as the Ghost Dance movement in the United States. There were dozens of such movements in South America, and a number among the Maori in New Zealand that still exist, such as the Ratana Church. And some Maori groups have revived traditional forms of communalism that they believe provide better lives for their people than can be achieved through integration into the larger society.

Thus, in the settler colonies of North and South America, Africa, Australia, and New Zealand we can follow a common story of utopian settlement destroying living, vital cultures with their own myths and stories that included utopian imagery, the continued dreaming of the settlers, the ending of colonialism, and the emergence of new dreams for both the descendants of the settlers and the descendants of the original inhabitants, and the rediscovery of the dreams of the cultures that had been suppressed.

At times, the cultures being destroyed were given a utopian hue by their oppressors. This was done in the Noble Savage tradition that, while it had parallels in peoples like the Scythians described by classical Greek and Roman writers, was most noteworthy after contact with the natives of North and South America. The Noble Savage was seen as closer to nature and, therefore, somehow purer, simpler, and better than the supposedly civilized. While obviously oversimplified, some contended that there was a truth hidden in the image. The American religious dissident Roger Williams (1603–83) reported an Indian saying: 'We wearne no Clothes, have many gods, And yet our sinnes are lesse: You are Barbarians, Pagans wild, *Your* Land's the Wilderness.'

But most of the utopian literature written by indigenous peoples are dystopias describing their treatment by the settlers both at the time of settlement and continuing to the present. For example, the Native American writer Leslie Marmon Silko's (b. 1948) *Gardens in the Dunes* (1999) contrasts the utopia of traditional American Indian life with the dystopia created by US policy; and 'The Farm' (1996) by Sherman Alexie (b. 1966), another Native American writer, describes a future United States of concentration camps for American Indians.

Involuntary immigration

Sometimes the settlement process was not voluntary. Africans were brought to the United States and South America as slaves, and convicts were transported to Australia and some French colonies, with the French transporting more slaves to their Caribbean colonies than were transported to either North or South America. Many stayed, but there were a number of slave revolts and the Haitian Revolution of 1791–1804 ended slavery in that country.

Those taken to the new place as slaves were rarely in a position to write down their visions of a better life, but that does not mean they did not have them, and they sang songs and told tales, some of which have survived. The best known are the spirituals of the slaves of the Southern United States, which regularly present images of the paradise they will win after the horrors of this life. Less well known are the stories of the 'great good place' told by the same people, stories directly parallel to the medieval Cockaigne or the tales of abundance told during the Great Depression. Food that comes without back-breaking labour, freedom from authority, and rest are central themes.

Also, due to the famine, the Irish diaspora was often involuntary, and Ireland is a special case both because, to many Irish, Ireland remains a colony because of Northern Ireland, and because, unlike most immigrants, the famine meant that it was difficult, if not impossible, to return if things did not work out in the new land. Thus, the Irish were in some ways more refugees than immigrants, and many kept moving from country to country before finally settling or coming to their end.

Israel/Palestine

A country that is rarely labelled a settler colony but clearly is one is Israel. Early Jewish utopian materials include the story of Eden in Genesis, the prophets, various texts not included in the Christian Old Testament including some apocalyptic books and texts describing the coming of a messiah, and the withdrawn religious community in Qumran and a similar community called the Therapeutae in Egypt. And in the 12th century, a Jewish author, Judah HaLevi, produced a book, *Kuzari: The Book of Argument and Proof*, that, along with two Islamic books from the same period, *Hayy Ibn Yaqzan* and *The Treatise of Kamil*, is among the earliest works describing someone living alone on an isolated island, an idea that later became popular with Daniel Defoe's *Robinson Crusoe*.

Many Jews believe that they have simply resettled land that was once theirs and that was given to them by their God, and this is reflected in a growing utopianism in Israel on the religious right which justifies their taking over houses and land owned, sometimes for generations, by Palestinians. But renewed Jewish settlement began as part of a series of explicitly utopian projects such as the writings of Theodor Herzl (1860–1904), including *Der Judenstaat* (*The Jewish State*; 1896) and *Altneuland* (*Oldnewland*; 1901), and the establishment of the first kibbutz in 1920. And it is the kibbutz movement that has most influenced 20th- and 21st-century utopianism, with the successes and failures of the kibbutz movement influencing intentional communities around the world.

On the other hand, most Palestinian utopianism takes one of two forms. For some, it is simply the desire of Palestinians for a land of their own or the return of the land they believe was theirs after having owned it for many, sometimes hundreds of, years. For others, their utopianism is simply a part of Islamism. I have been told of the existence of some Palestinian utopias from the first half

of the 20th century, but none appears to exist in any European or
North American library.

Independence

Some settler colonies opted for complete independence, like the
USA, Brazil, and the Spanish colonies of Latin and South America,
and some opted to keep ties, gradually loosening, with the colonial
power, like Australia, Canada, and New Zealand. But in a
fascinating twist, both the independence movements where they
existed and the movements for recognition and rights in the settler
colonies have used the language of the home country and the
settlers, including their utopian language, against them. It was
standard practice to say something like, 'If you believe what you
say you believe, you cannot continue to treat us as you have. We
are only asking for what you say to be right.' As a result, both
indigenous and colonial utopias have played a role in the
postcolonial period.

The United States

One of the very first successful colonies was one where economic
factors were not among the first priorities of the colonists. That was
the colony established at Plymouth in 1620 in what became the
state of Massachusetts. There, religious considerations were
foremost; the colonists wanted to be able to practise the way of
life that they believed their religion required. For example, John
Winthrop (1588–1649), the first governor of Massachusetts Bay
Colony, said that the Puritans had travelled to America to build a
'citty upon a hill'. While Winthrop was actually warning his people
that 'the eyes of all people are upon us' and meant his statement
as a warning against failure, it is now read as a statement of early
American utopianism.

The freedom to practise their religious beliefs did not extend to
allowing others to practise their beliefs. The Society of Friends, or
Quakers, who settled in Pennsylvania were the first colonists who

settled for religious reasons who practised religious freedom in what became the United States. The third colony that was established primarily for religious reasons was Maryland, which was settled by Roman Catholics.

The colonies of South Carolina and Georgia included specific utopian plans, although they were not carried out. In South Carolina, Lord Ashley, the 1st Earl of Shaftesbury (1621–83), collaborating with the philosopher and political theorist John Locke (1632–1704), designed what they called the 'Fundamental Constitutions', which proposed a semi-feudal aristocracy with a new American nobility. In Georgia, the Scotsman Sir Robert Montgomery (c. 1680–1731) developed a plan for a utopia called Azilia, and German missionary Christian Priber (1697–1744) tried to establish utopian communities among the Indians. Later, the actual founding of the colony of Georgia under the British general James Oglethorpe (1686–1785) was designed for paupers and debtors as well as to make a profit for the landowners.

The other early American colonies were primarily designed to make a profit for the holders of the land grants, but holding out the hope of a better life for the settlers was one aspect of how they intended to profit. As with most such settlement, that better life was to be the result of very hard work for many years as the settler slowly accumulated the money that would permit the purchase of land or the establishment of a shop or trade.

Many early US immigrants came as what were called 'indentured servants' who had contracted themselves to a certain number of years' service in exchange for their passage over. While some bosses did their best to ensure that such service never ended, and some indentured servants ran away (the seemingly empty land to the west was always a temptation), for most the system worked as intended and after working off their indenture, they worked on their own behalf until they could buy land or set themselves up independently in a shop or trade. Of course, some failed, but there were real opportunities for betterment. Similar practices existed in many colonies because the cost of passage was well beyond the resources of the people most desperate to leave.

Of course, some were better off and therefore able to establish themselves more easily. For example, J. Hector St John de Crèvecoeur (1735–1813) settled in what became the United States in 1759, adopted the name John Hector St John on becoming a citizen, married, bought a farm, and set about to farm and to write about the experience. In 1782, he published *Letters from an American Farmer* (with expanded versions in 1784 and 1787) in which he described America for a European audience in nearly utopian terms. Crèvecoeur's *Letters* was less positive in the later editions, but such utopian descriptions by settlers became a standard fare and helped attract immigrants to most settler colonies. In some cases, land agents published fictional descriptions and fictional letters home to attract immigrants.

The early utopias in the settler colonies often dealt with practical issues like the distribution of land and the structure of government. At the end of the colonial period, as the American colonies separated from Britain and became the United States of America, three documents were created, two of which have served to inspire utopias both in the USA and elsewhere. The first, the Declaration of Independence, asserted liberty and equality and justified revolution. The second of the three documents, the Articles of Confederation, is largely forgotten and has generally been written off as a failure because it provided for only a weak central government and left most power in the individual states, but it was under the Articles that the USA successfully fought the Revolution, established diplomatic relations, and expanded the territory of the country. The third document, the United States Constitution, usually called the first written constitution by ignoring the Articles, has served as a model for many other constitutions. After the Constitution was ratified, ten amendments, known as the Bill of Rights, were added, and those amendments

8. The Declaration of Independence declared the independence of the thirteen American colonies from British rule. It asserted the people have 'certain unalienable rights' and asserts a right of revolution

have become a central utopian document in the USA. The idea that the structure of government and the rights and duties of both citizens and governments should be spelled out has inspired many utopian constitutions and bills of rights as well as many that have been implemented.

Canada, Australia, and New Zealand

In Canada, the relation between the English and the French was particularly important in early Canadian utopias and continues to be a central issue in French Canada. For example, an early English-language Canadian utopia, *The Young Seigneur; or, Nation-Making* by Wilfrid Châteauclair (1888) uses a half English and half French pseudonym and is directly concerned with English–French relations. And the very first French-Canadian utopia, 'Mon voyage à la lune', published under the pseudonym Napoléon Aubin (1839), focuses on independence from English Canada.

In Australia, a constant theme was what to do with the vast empty middle of the country and the generally harsh landscape, with constant fires and drought alternating with floods – issues that still exist. This produced what may be the first dystopia of global warming, 'The Fool and His Inheritance' (1911) by James Edmond (1859–1933), a long-serving editor of the Australian journal *The Bulletin*.

New Zealand utopias, such as Alexander Joyce's (1840/41–1927) *Land Ho!! A Conversation of 1933* (1881), dealt most often with land redistribution and other means of achieving greater equality. At the same time, many early New Zealand utopias simply depicted New Zealand itself as a utopia. For example, early utopian poems like 'The Avon' (1854) by Henry Jacobs (1824–1901) and 'There's Nae Place Like Otago Yet' (1861) by John Barr of Craigielee (1809–89) both depict parts of New Zealand, Canterbury and Otago respectively, as ready-made utopias, and that approach continued well into the late 20th century.

Latin and South America

Political literature in Latin and South America was initially concerned with independence and, although there were some exceptions, specifically utopian literature was relatively slow to appear. When it did, it was concerned with the same issues as in the other settler colonies, with disparities of wealth and poverty being the most common. As time passed, the issues initially changed little, but the sophistication of the utopias grew along with their numbers, and in the late 20th century indigenous peoples also began to write utopias, and they mostly wrote dystopias fictionally depicting their treatment by the settlers.

During the period of colonization, relations between the colonizers and the indigenous population were frequently violent, but there were attempts, sometimes based directly on More's *Utopia*, to develop better relations. While these attempts look less positive through 21st-century eyes than they did to their founders, they were examples of a paternalistic utopianism that, despite differences in the actual institutions, had similarities to More's vision.

Bartolomé de las Casas (1484–1566), a Spanish Dominican, wrote *Remedios para las Indias* (*Memorial of Remedies for the Indies*; 1516), which may have influenced More. He also tried to establish a community in Venezuela that would have had Spanish farmers teaching current agricultural techniques to the natives, who would have been paid a fair wage rather than being enslaved, which was the norm. The idea was to Christianize and civilize the Indians while improving relations between the colonizers and the colonized.

In 1552 and 1553, Vasco de Quiroga (1470–1565), a Spanish layman who was appointed the first bishop of Michoacán in Mexico, established pueblo-hospitals or communal towns in Santa Fe de Mexico near Mexico City and Santa Fe de la Laguna outside Michoacán. The communities were directly based on his reading of More's *Utopia* and were intended to improve the lives of the

Indians while Christianizing them. Both communities, but particularly the one outside Michoacán, lasted for some time and were successful on both their economic and religious dimensions.

In the 17th and 18th centuries, the Jesuits established 'reductions', or communities designed to Christianize, govern, and educate the peoples of the area. Such 'reductions' were established in Argentina, Bolivia, Brazil, and Paraguay and existed as communities until the Jesuits were forced out of these areas.

South Africa

South Africa was late in producing utopian literature and when it came it was primarily concerned with racial issues, with much such literature justifying and defending racial separation. Examples include James Marshall and Margaret Scott Marshall's *1960 (A Retrospect)* (1912) in English and *Na die geliefde* (1972) by Karel Schoeman in Afrikaans.

But others presented a more complex picture, and Nadine Gordimer (b. 1923, Nobel Prize for Literature 1991) wrote a number of novels about what she called 'the interregnum' between white dominance and the coming change that were most often set a short way into the future. These novels, like her 1981 *July's People* and 1987 *A Sport of Nature*, depict the entire range of racial relations in South Africa, sometimes expanded to other parts of Africa, but stressing that change was coming and that, while the direction of change was problematic, the current dystopia could be improved.

When the change came, the first issue to be dealt with was the need for a new constitution, and many South Africans believe that the document is truly utopian even if its implementation has not been, and indeed is seen as dystopian by many. Today, many South Africans, black, white, and coloured, are deeply unhappy with the pace and/or direction of change, and a few post-Apartheid South African works have been published that are concerned with the future. Most, as in the rest of the world, are dystopian, and some, such as *South Africa 1994-2004* (1991) published under the pseudonym Tom Barnard, *Jacob with a 'C'* (1993) by Edward Lurie, and *The Mask of Freedom* (1994) by Peter Wilhelm (b. 1943), present a future in which South Africa has reverted to racial separation.

Postcolonial utopianism

Although very few colonies in the old sense still exist, immigration continues as people search for better lives. The fact that today's immigrants are often disparagingly called 'economic immigrants' by the descendants of earlier immigrants ignores the fact that immigration almost always had an economic dimension even though in specific instances other factors were of equal or greater importance.

Postcolonial utopianism in settler colonies is somewhat different from postcolonial utopianism in those colonies that were primarily designed to exploit their human and material resources. While the descendants of the original inhabitants were using the settler utopias to justify change, in some countries the descendants of the settlers were beginning to learn about and incorporate the myths, including the utopian ones, of the original inhabitants in their new utopias. In the exploitative colonies, the same use was made of the political traditions of the colonial power to justify independence, but the utopias that developed, which are discussed in the next chapter, are directly concerned with local issues, particularly the problems that came with independence.

Utopian experiments

Settler colonies became places of utopian experimentation. From as early as 1659, intentional communities were established within the American colonies. While the first such community was founded in Delaware by the Dutchman Pieter Plockhoy (c. 1629-c. 1700) and practised religious freedom, most of the earliest ones were founded by Germans, like the Ephrata community in Pennsylvania, and were religious without internal religious freedom.

The 1917 constitution in Mexico promised to restore a system of communal land use that Mexicans traced back to the Aztecs. In the *ejidos*, the government owns the land but it is used communally and, under reforms instituted in the 1930s, the farmers had a right of use as long as the land was actually used, and that right could be passed on to their children. The constitutional right was abolished in the 1990s but some *ejidos* still exist.

There have never been a lot of South American intentional communities, but such communities have existed or exist today in Brazil, Chile, Columbia, Ecuador, and Paraguay. Colonia Dignidad in Chile was a dystopian community established in 1961 whose leader was jailed for child sex abuse and who apparently allowed the military regime under General Augusto Pinochet (1915–2006) to use its facilities to torture its opponents.

Paraguay has attracted a number of communities to settle there from other countries. In the late 19th century, Nueva Germania was established with the idea of creating a pure Aryan community; descendants still live in the area. About the same time, the Australian labour leader William Lane (1861–1917) and his followers established New Australia and Cosme. While the communities did not last long, and Lane and many others returned to Australia, there are descendants of the Australians still living in the region. And in the 1920s, Mennonites from Europe and North America settled in Paraguay and established communities that still exist.

Australia became a centre for the garden city movement, which originated with the English utopia *To-Morrow: A Peaceful Path to Real Reform* (1898), better known as *Garden Cities of To-Morrow* (1902), by Ebenezer Howard (1850–1928). Garden cities were established in many countries, such as Letchworth Garden City and Welwyn Garden City in England and Radburn, New Jersey, in the USA. But Australia appears to have had more than any other country, and also has more intentional communities per capita than any country other than Israel. New Zealand also has a very strong tradition of intentional communities.

Communities come in all types, including very tightly closed-off religious communities such as Gloriavale in New Zealand and secular communities open to new members and visits from outsiders, like Twin Oaks in the USA, and they vary in size from under a dozen members to hundreds of members. There are communities that trace their ancestry back hundreds of years, existing communities that have been in the same place nearly a hundred years, and those founded last week, with many proposed communities looking to become established.

Chapter 4
Utopianism in other traditions

People on the Northern Island '... make no use of agriculture or any other art or profession. A tree named Padesà grows in that fortunate island on which, instead of fruit, are seen hanging precious garments of various colours, whereof the natives take whatever pleases them best. In like manner they need not cultivate the soil, nor sow, nor reap; neither do they fish, nor hunt; because the same tree naturally produces them an excellent kind of rice without any husk. Whenever they wish to take nourishment, they have only to place this rice upon a certain great stone, from which a flame instantly issues, dresses their food, and then goes out of itself. While they eat their rice, various kinds of exquisite meats, ready dressed, appear upon the leaves of some trees, from which everyone takes at will. The meal over the remains immediately disappear.'

(Burmese Buddhist text, quoted by Father Sangermano)

Take a small country with a small population. The sage could bring it about that though there were contrivances which saved labour ten or a hundred times over, the people would not use them. He could make the people ready to die twice over for their country rather than emigrate. There might still be boats and chariots but no one would ride in them. There

ought still be weapons of war but no one would drill with
them. He could bring it about that 'the people should go
back (from writing) to knotted cords, be contented with their
food, pleased with their clothes, satisfied with their homes,
and happy in their work and customs. The country over the
border might be so near that one could hear the cocks
crowing and the dogs barking in it, but the people would
grow old and die without ever once troubling to go there.'

(*Tao Te Ching*, quoted by Joseph Needham)

Krishan Kumar, the author of *Utopia and Anti-Utopia in Modern
Times* (1987), argues that utopias are a phenomenon of the West,
that they emerged from Christianity, and that there are no
non-Western utopian traditions that did not arise from contact
with Western utopias. Today, most scholars disagree and argue
that such traditions existed in most cultures, noting such traditions
in Buddhist, Confucian, and Taoist China, Buddhist and Hindu
India, the Islamic countries of the Middle East, Buddhist
Southeast Asia, and Buddhist and Shinto Japan.

Thomas More invented a literary genre, but there are numerous
texts both in the West and outside it that pre-date More's *Utopia*
that describe a non-existent society identifiably better than the
contemporary society. Thus it is clear that utopian traditions that
pre-date More existed outside the West. Following contact with
Western utopianism, all these areas, plus the cultures of Africa,
began to produce utopias using the model that More invented but
adapting it to their specific circumstances. As a result, their utopias
both address their own issues and are often significantly different
in form and content from the utopias that developed in the West
after 1516.

As can be seen from the quotations at the head of the chapter,
although there are important cultural differences, there are
similarities among the myths. There are two common utopian

forms with parallels in the West that are found in most cultures: an ideal society in the past and some version of paradise. In particular, the image of there being a utopian period in the past is very common and central to utopianism in most cultures. In Burma, before it became Myanmar, both the constitution and the law code included prefaces that explicitly connected the modern legal system with the utopia that was believed to have existed in the past. Thus, in Burma the utopian past remained a touchstone of life until the late 20th century.

The greatest difference between the Christian utopian past of Eden and the other myths is that there is no Fall. There is always some explanation for why the utopian past ended, but never the sort of complete break which the Fall represents. As a result, utopianism is not heretical. The other myths also differ from the Greek myth of the golden age in that in the Greek myth there is a series of separate creations that lead to the development of the non-utopian present, while in the other cultures there are no separate creations and no clean break. This means that the utopian past is not necessarily lost and can be used as a model for the future. This is particularly important in China because the belief is that both the Confucian and Taoist utopias had once actually existed, and therefore they could exist again if the principles on which they were based are rightly understood and then put into practice.

China

Chinese utopianism is the best known of the traditions outside the West. It has roots in Confucianism, Taoism, and Buddhism, followed by Neo-Confucianism and, in more popular form, various dissident groups. Chinese utopian fiction became popular in the 19th and 20th centuries, although beginning earlier, and dystopian literature developed in the 20th century. And there was a strong utopian element in the Communism of Mao Zedong, even though the result of Mao's policies was dystopian for many.

Early Confucian, Taoist, and Buddhist utopianism differed in that the Taoist utopia, which is often called 'The Great Peace', was initially opposed to government in all forms and could be called anarchist – and Taoism is today often called anarchist. All three traditions look back to a time in the past when rulership was not necessary and people lived simply in harmony with nature. This utopia gradually came to focus on the need for wise men (and here the masculine is correct) to provide guidance, and Confucians in particular always looked back to this period as an ideal to be recreated in the present. One element of the Confucian utopia was a stress on self-improvement, and this emphasis and the concern with wise men were the bases for the role education played in Chinese society as the primary means of upward mobility (although the concern with wisdom was replaced by the ability to pass exams).

One other early utopian proposal was the 'well-field' system, which proposed the egalitarian distribution of land and was even presented as having existed in the past and capable of being put into practice again. The idea is that if everyone has a piece of land, everyone will be able to support themselves. While the 'well-field' system probably did not exist in the past, it was seriously presented as a possibility between the late BCE and the early CE.

The Book of Poetry, the earliest record of Chinese literature, contains a poem, generally called 'Big Rat', that suggests that the people will be able find a better place to live than where they currently live. But the classic Chinese utopia is 'The Peach Blossom Spring' by T'ao Yüan-ming (365–427). In this story, one day a fisherman went up an unfamiliar stream and came across a peach orchard in full bloom on both sides of the stream; intoxicated by its beauty, he continued up the stream until he came to a small cave from which the stream issued. He entered the cave and squeezing through the small opening came out on an open plain dotted with simple houses and fine fields and ponds, and all the inhabitants that he observed were clearly happy. They took him home and fed him and told him that they had escaped from the turmoil of the early Ch'in dynasty, about 600 years before the tale is set, and their ancestors had settled in this isolated place and kept themselves cut off from the rest of the world. After staying for some days, the fisherman chose to leave. He was encouraged not to tell anyone outside about the place. When he got home, he told the authorities of the place, but no one was ever able to find it.

This story influenced later Chinese literature and was reproduced in Japan, with the Japanese word for 'Peach Blossom Spring' coming to be the equivalent of Shangri-la. In China, an 8th-century book, *Kuang-i chi*, used a similar approach to describe visits to a land of Taoist immortals and a group of women who had escaped from the labour gang being forced to build the Great Wall and who established a utopian society in an isolated valley where they became immortal.

Chinese utopian fiction developed in the 18th century, with the most famous work being *Flowers in the Mirror* (1828) by Li Ju-chen (1760?–1830?). This book is a bit like *Gulliver's Travels* in that a number of countries are visited, such as *Chun-tzu Kuo*, or the Country of Gentlemen, and *Ta-jen Kuo*, or the Country of Great Men, but the visit that has gained the most attention is that to *Nu-erh Kuo*, or the Country of Women, where women hold all the power and women are educated in the same way men were elsewhere. While the 'Country of Women' is seen as an early statement on women's rights, it was not until the 20th century that a number of feminist utopias were published in China.

In the 19th and the early 20th centuries, Chinese utopias tended to focus on the desirability of adopting Western technology, but keeping Chinese morality to soften the impact of the technology, and in the 20th century dystopias developed that rejected Western technology. And the social philosopher K'ang Yu-wei (1858–1927) wrote a number of utopian works accepting Western technology and describing a democratic world state based on far-reaching

9. Confucius presenting the young Gautama Buddha to Laozi, the author of the *Tao Te Ching*, so that here are depicted the founders of the three ways of thinking that dominated ancient China

equality. There would be a world parliament which would, among its normal legislative duties, develop a universal language and oversee the gradual reduction of armed forces throughout the world. Capitalism, and all private property, would be abolished, and K'ang's utopia stressed the need to change the status of women, which would require, among other things, the abolition of lifelong marriage and the institution of limited-term contracts between men and women.

In the 20th century, a number of authors presented ideal constitutions for a future China, such as *Hsin Chung-kuo Wei-lai Chi* (*The Future of New China*; 1902) by Liang Chi-chiao (1873–1929); *Shih-tzu Hou* (*The Lion Roars*; 1905–6) by Ch'en Tien-hua; and the anonymous *Hsien Chih Hun* (*The Soul of the Constitution*; 1907). Also in 20th-century China, Mao Zedong was clearly utopian in his desire to transform Chinese society along the lines of his vision for it, and it can be argued that Mao's Communism was both Marxist and rooted in Confucianism.

India

The fundamental texts of traditional Indian religions point to a golden age in the past and trace the gradual changes and lapses in human behaviour that lead to the growth of social differences and the need for rulership. And these descriptions of periods of peace and prosperity in the past, although including elements of fantasy such as ever-renewing crops, are basic to religious, social, and political movements today.

In the late 19th and early 20th centuries, two Indian authors, Hara Prasad Shastri (1853–1931), a man and a Hindu, and Rokeya Sakhawat Hossain (1880–1932), a woman and a Muslim, published utopias. Shastri's *Valmikir Jaya* (*The Triumph of Valmiki*) was probably published in the late 1870s or early 1880s and in English in 1909 and presents the Hindu earthly paradise as a modern utopia. Hossain's 'Sultana's Dream' (1905) was written

and published in English and her *Padmarag* (1924) was
written and published in Bengali. Both are feminist utopias.
'Sultana's Dream' describes Ladyland, a country of women, and
Padmarag, which is mostly concerned with the terrible conditions
of Indian women of the time, describes a community of women
who provide a school for girls, a refuge for abused women, and a
hospital for female patients. A school for girls that Hossain
founded in 1910 still exists.

Mohandas K. Gandhi (1869–1948) was a utopian and used the
Hindu notion of Ramaraja, or the rule of Rama, the golden age, as
a means of communicating his ideas. Gandhi looked back to what
he believed to be the structure of early Indian civilization as the
basis of the utopia he hoped to bring about in modern India.

Gandhi directly contrasted his vision of the past/future with the
dystopia, both capitalist and socialist, that he saw in the materialist
and competitive West because, for Gandhi, the foundation of
utopia must rest on spirituality. Gandhi's utopia was to be based on
small communities in which each of the main groups, or *varna*, of
Indian society would fulfil its defined role in cooperation with all of
the other groups. This small community would be governed by the
village elders, or *panchayat*, speaking for the entire community.
Gandhi's most radical revision of this cooperative structure was that
it would include rather than exclude the Dalit, or 'untouchables',
and Dalits would be guaranteed seats in parliament by the Indian
constitution. Life would be simple, with all people collectively
producing what they need. Gandhi himself famously wove cloth.

The principles behind Gandhi's utopia were, first, *Swaraj*, or
self-control/individual discipline, with a nation achieving *Swaraj*
to the extent that its individual citizens did. The second principle
was *Ahimsa*, or a respect for life. Third was *satyagraha*, which
can be translated as 'truth force', and by which Gandhi meant the
positive practice of non-violence. And fourth was trusteeship
socialism, or a socialism without class differences, and in this

Gandhi was a forerunner of socialist theorists such as Léopold Sédar Senghor (1906–2001) of Senegal, Julius K. Nyerere (1922–99) of Tanzania, and U Nu (1907–95) of Burma, with the Indian version being developed by Gandhi's follower Vinoba Bhave (1895–1982).

Today, India has a utopian movement that is close to the centres of political power. The Hindutva movement wants to destroy the religious plurality of India and establish, or as the movement would put it, re-establish, India as a purely Hindu nation. The targets of the Hindutva movement are Muslims and Christians, and it has used legal and political power as well as violence against these targets.

Japan

There is real disagreement over the existence of a native Japanese utopianism. Japanese myth either does or does not include utopias. If it does, the utopias were or were not borrowed from China. And the argument continues to the present day, with Japanese utopias either slavishly imitative or very original.

The answer to the problem is, as so often, found between the extremes. There is a strong Japanese utopian tradition, some of which was deeply influenced by China, and later by Europe and the USA, but a substantial amount of it was radically modified to fit the Japanese situation. For example, the first Japanese translation of Thomas More's *Utopia* as *On Good Government* (1892) was not in fact a translation but an adaptation to fit Japan and was designed to be used by the Japanese to inspire social change.

The Japanese word for utopia is *riso-kyo*, which derived from an earlier word *tokoyo*, or a world that exists forever. *Tokoyo* was used as early as the 8th century to describe the Taoist world of immortals, which in both Chinese and Japanese traditions has been presented as a utopia. And *Tokoyo no Kuni* refers to the fifth part of the Shinto cosmos which is located across the seas and is utopian. And there is a Japanese tradition of looking to the past for utopia in the hope of recreating it in the future.

Japan was deeply influenced by Buddhism as well as Taoism, but both were modified in Japan. Certain aspects of Taoism were incorporated into Shinto, and Japan developed its own version of Buddhism, Zen Buddhism, which was later influential in the West, where it is considered the most sophisticated form of Buddhism. The Zen ethos is often represented in the West by the austerity and simplicity of a stone garden. Susan J. Napier, a scholar of Japanese literature at Tufts University, has argued that there is a traditional Japanese aesthetic utopia, which can even be found in that classic of Japanese literature, *The Tale of Genji* (11th century).

10. The Zen gardens differ from most gardens in being composed primarily of stones and sand. The gardens reflect a Japanese artform, and the maintenance of the garden and the process of raking it helps the monks concentrate and meditate

Others have argued that the Japanese art of *ukiyo* can be seen as an aesthetic utopia depicting fleeting pleasures and ephemeral beauty.

At the same time, a more traditional Buddhism can be found in Japanese Buddhist paradises, which include extremely complex cities. Some Japanese Buddhism, like some Indian and Chinese Buddhism, was based on the expectation of the *Miroku* or Maitreya, the future Buddha who will come at some future date to revitalize Buddhism.

One popular story, 'Taketori monogatari' or 'The Tale of the Bamboo Cutter', from the late 9th or early 10th century, in which a visitor from the moon rewards a human for his assistance, is often considered an early Japanese utopia. But the most common early Japanese utopias are works influenced by the Peach Blossom Spring, which was adapted slightly in Japan. For example, in 'The Story of Urashima Taró', a fisher boy saves a turtle from other boys and is rewarded with a trip to a paradise-like world. On his return, he discovers that he has been gone for ages rather than the few days he thought, which is a standard feature of such tales in most cultures.

Thus, there are traditional Japanese myths with utopian content and at least a few early Japanese tales with some utopian content, both derived from Chinese sources but modified in Japan. But most Japanese utopias have been published after contact with Europe and the USA, and a Japanese utopian literature did not emerge quickly. In the 17th century, there was a slight piece by Ihara Saikaku (1642–93) called *The Life of an Amorous Man* (1682) which, while predominantly depicting a group of men who lived solely for pleasure, ends with them going in search of the 'Isle of Nyogo', an isolated island inhabited solely by strong women. In the 18th century, there were various travel fantasies, including at least one based on Swift's *Gulliver's Travels*. And Andō Shōeki

(1701–58) included a section in his *Shizen shin'eidō* (1775) that describes a simple, natural, self-sufficient utopia.

In the late 19th century, under the influence of the popular novels of Jules Verne (1828–1905) and then of H. G. Wells, Japanese science fiction began to develop, first as political novels projecting the future and then as technological futures, initially primarily utopian and then, as elsewhere, dystopian, with, in some cases, attacks on the West as the ultimate dystopia. Most recently, Japanese *manga* (graphic novels) frequently depict a dystopian future or, much more rarely, a positive utopian one.

Islam

Historically, Islam has a limited utopian tradition, but with two basic utopias, paradise and the early Muslim community at Medina. The Medina period of peace before the move to Mecca and the need to fight to defend the faith is the golden age of Islam. In fact, some Muslim scholars, such as the Sudanese politician and theologian Mahmoud Mohamed Taha (1909–1985), argue that the Qu'ran should be read as reflecting two very different periods, Medina and Mecca, with the Medina texts the most important. While this is a decidedly minority viewpoint, the period in Medina, before the warfare and the schisms that created the two major sects of Sunni and Shiite, as well as a number of smaller splinter groups, plays a special role in the Islamic imagination.

The Ruba'iyat of Omar Khayyam (1048–1131) has been described as the first Persian utopia and in the best-known English translation, by Edward Fitzgerald, that is a good description. Well-known passages like 'A Book of Verses underneath the Bough, A Jug of Wine, a Loaf of Bread – and Thou Beside me singing in the Wilderness – Oh, Wilderness were Paradise now!' give us a pleasure-oriented utopia. But Fitzgerald adapted rather than translated, and verses such as that quoted do not reflect the whole book, which is more like *Ecclesiastes* with its emphasis on the fact of death as the end of all our pleasures, and while there are passages in *The Ruba'iyat* that stress pleasure and sexual desire, the emphasis is on the oblivion found in wine, a most un-Islamic emphasis.

Two other works from roughly the same time more accurately reflect Islamic beliefs. *Hayy Ibn Yaqzan: A Philosophical Tale*, from around 1150, and *The Treatise of Kamil on the Prophet's Biography*, from about 100 years later, use the device of a child alone on an isolated island to demonstrate that the human mind can itself deduce religious truths, those truths being the essentials of Islam.

Today, Islam, while often seen by outsiders as a single, coherent belief system, is in fact deeply divided, with liberal, feminist, and even some gay and lesbian Muslims arguing for the interpretation of the Qu'ran that supports their position at one extreme, and fundamental Islamists arguing for their interpretation at the other, with the vast majority of believers in the middle. While Islamists disagree among themselves, they all want to establish the *Shari'a* (Islamic law) as the basis of the social order, and they are the most utopian Muslims today. The vision of the Islamic Republic developed for Iran by Ayatollah Ruhollah Khomeini (1900–89) and by the Taliban for Afghanistan were clearly utopian, and some of Khomeini's publications, such as *Kashf al-Asrar* (*The Unveiling of Secrets*; 1944) and *Hokomat-Eslami* (*The Islamic Government*; 1971), while treatises, give detailed descriptions of the ideal Islamic society as he saw it, and of course he then gained the power to try to put his beliefs into effect.

There is little evidence of fictional descriptions of the Islamist utopia, but there are at least two such works. *Al-bu'd al-khāmas* (*The Fifth Dimension*) is a play written in an Egyptian prison, where the author had been sent for his involvement with the Muslim Brotherhood. The utopia appears to be based on the teachings of Sayyid Qutb (1906–66), one of the theorists of Islamism. The other work, *Barnameh-ye Fada'ian-Eslam*

(The Revolutionary Programme of Fada'ian-e Elam; 1950) by the Iranian Seyyed Mojtaba Navvab Safavi (b. 1924, executed 1955) outlined an ideal Islamic social system. It is a very simple, even simplistic, amalgam of Islamic theology and moral rules.

Africa

The Kenyan literary critic Simon Gikandi says that the focus of the African novel is 'the problematic of [state] power'. Many African utopias read as if they were realistic novels about the dystopias that exist in their homelands under either civilian or military dictatorships. They are set apart primarily by being set in imaginary countries or in the near future. But quite a few African novelists have written positive utopias. Bessie Head's (1937–86) *When Rain Clouds Gather* (1969) is her most explicitly utopian work and presents the attempt to create a utopian village, but her *Maru* (1971) and *A Question of Power* (1974) both present African village life in generally positive terms. Ayi Kwei Armah (b. 1939) wrote both a utopia and a dystopia. His *Two Thousand Seasons* (1973) presents a re-envisioned past of Africa as an egalitarian utopia, but his *The Beautyful Ones Are Not Yet Born* (1968) is similar to other African dystopias in presenting the contemporary situation in one country, the Congo in this case, as a dystopia. Wole Soyinka (b. 1934) presents both utopia and dystopia in one novel. The first two chapters of his *Season of Anomy* (1973) present a communal utopia, but much of the rest of the book presents current reality as dystopia. Still the utopian country of Aiyéró provides the possibility of something better. And from Mali, there is Djibril Tamsir Niane's (b. 1932) *Soundjata: ou, L'epopee mandinique* (*Sundiata: An Epic of Old Mali*; 1960), which is presented as the oral history of one of the kings of Mali and ends with the utopia his success brought about when there was peace and prosperity.

In addition to those already mentioned, African utopias include, from Kenya, *The Trial of Christopher Okigbo* (1971) by Ali A. Mazrui (b. 1933); Ngũgĩ wa Thiong'o's (b. 1938) *Petals of Blood*

11. Chinua Achebe (b. 1930) is a Nigerian writer from the Igbo tribe who has taught in Nigeria and the United States. He is best known for his satires on contemporary African life

(1977), *Devil on the Cross* (1980), and *Murogi wa Kagogo* (*Wizard of the Crow*; 2004). From Nigeria, there is *The Rape of Shavi* (1983) by Buchi Emechta (b. 1944); *Anthills of the Savannah* by Chinua Achebe (b. 1930); and *Astonishing the Gods* (1995) and *In*

Arcadia (2002) by Ben Okri (b. 1959). From Ghana; there is *Woman of the Aeroplanes* (1988) and *Major Gentl and the Achimota War* (1992) by Kojo Laing (b. 1946); and *Black Fury* (1995) by Kodwo Abaidoo. And from Senegal, there is *Le dernier de L'Empire* (*The Last of the Empire: A Senegalese Novel*; 1980) by Sembène Ousmane (1923–2007).

Intentional communities

Buddhist monasteries in India, China, Japan, and Southeast Asia had flourished from as early as 500 BCE. Ashrams, which are dwelling places for those living some form of spiritual discipline in India and emerging from Hinduism, had an even longer history, being traced back to around 1500 BCE. Thus, just as Christian monasticism is now considered a part of the long history on intentional communities in the West and precursors to modern intentional communities, so the traditions in these areas continue to flourish, are part and parcel of local culture, and have spread to other areas through immigration.

Recently, India has developed Christian ashrams attracting Christian Indians to communalism in parallel to the traditional Hindu ashrams. But these Christian ashrams are under some threat from the Hindutva movement.

India and Japan in particular have seen the development in modern times of a significant number of both religious and secular intentional communities, and some of these, like Auroville in India, have been influential throughout the intentional community movement. Auroville was founded in 1968 and is currently home to around 2,000 people, which probably makes it the largest intentional community in the world, and it employs a total of around 4,000 people.

Today, outside those involved in the intentional community movement, Indian communalism is likely to be identified with

Indian movements that moved outside India and which many would label cults, like the followers of the Shree Baghwan Rajneesh (1931–90) who established communities in the UK and the USA, most notably in Oregon, where, after conflict with the local governments of the area, they were closed down and their leader was expelled from the country. But probably the most familiar group today is the International Society for Krishna Consciousness (ISKON), or the Hare Krishna movement, whose members can be seen dancing, parading, and chanting in their colourful robes in most large cities.

Japan has a particularly rich communal history. In addition to Buddhist monasteries, particularly Zen monasteries that attracted many Westerners and have spread throughout the world, Japan has a strong cooperative movement. It has been influenced by the writings of Robert Owen, and there is a long-established Robert Owen Association of Japan. Japan also had as many as 300 cooperative villages in the 1970s. The idea of the garden city was very popular in pre-war Japan, but the idea was generally misunderstood, so that what were built and called garden cities were in fact standard suburban towns and did not reflect the concept as created by Ebenezer Howard.

Japan also developed its own indigenous communities, including dystopian cults like Aum Shinrikyō, which launched a poison attack on the Tokyo subway in 1995. The oldest Japanese commune, Ittō-En, or Garden of Light, was founded in 1911 and moved to its current location in 1928. Atarashiki Mura, or New Village, was founded in 1918 and other communities have been established on a regular basis from then to the present, with an upsurge in the 1970s that paralleled the upsurge in many other countries. Most of the Japanese communities were established around a charismatic leader, but some have survived the death of that leader.

China has a long tradition of Buddhist monasticism, and Christian monasteries were introduced together with Christianity, but the

12. A Hare Krishna group dancing on Oxford Street in London in 1980

conflicts of the 20th century meant that all religious institutions came under attack from the Communist government and many were destroyed forcibly or closed, and some are only now re-opening.

Otherwise, Chinese communalism in the 20th century tends to be identified with the forced communalism of the 1960s and 1970s, during which the government moved large numbers of people from their home villages to communal settlements. These were intentional communities in the sense that it was the government's intention to establish them; they were not intentional communities in the sense that the people in them were not there by their own choice. Temporarily, these communities appeared to fulfil the government's purposes of greater efficiency in food production, population distribution, use of labour (by freeing women to work by providing communal cooking and child care), the ability to harness labour for infrastructure projects, better housing and sanitation, and so forth, but they fairly quickly proved to be much less efficient than hoped and much less well planned than they needed to have been. Thus, while the traditional religious intentional communities are reviving, the 'Chinese commune' will not.

While there have been a few exceptions, African intentional communities have been almost entirely the result of the process of colonization, with European communitarians believing that Africa provided a place to put their ideas into practice, somehow managing to forget that the land was already occupied. The earliest of these was a proposal to settle Sierra Leone presented in the 1789 *Plan for a Free Community upon the Coast of Africa, Under the Protection of Great Britain; But Intirely Independent of all European Laws and Governments*. Nothing came of this, but various attempts to settle ex-slaves from Britain, Canada, and the USA in Sierra Leone were made, with only limited success. About a century later, Theodor Hertzka proposed establishing his Freiland community in Africa and gained much initial support.

None of these proposals amounted to much, but an experiment that was a success of sorts and included both broadly utopian proposals and some intentional communities was the settlement of Liberia by freed US slaves under the auspices of various US churches and, at times, with official support. The utopian novel *Liberia; or Mr. Peyton's Experiments* (1853) was written to support the project.

There is no tradition of Islamic communalism, but a few urban and rural intentional communities were established in the USA by African-American converts to Islam in the 1970s.

Global perspective

Thus, utopianism is not just a phenomenon of the Christian West, but exists in various forms in most, if not all, cultures. Myths of an early utopian age were the norm, with differences about what went wrong and whether or not such a utopia could be recovered or recreated. Visions of the good life to be brought about by human effort were also common and culturally specific. After More's *Utopia* became known, literary utopias using his model have been published throughout the world, but again they reflect the specific places in which they were written. At the same time, different countries and cultures often faced similar problems, and sometimes similar answers were produced. And social movements like feminism and environmentalism have raised questions that have been answered in similar ways in different places. But also different places have produced dissimilar answers to the problems raised, answers clearly reflecting local conditions.

Religious intentional communities appear to have emerged independently in many places and have reflected local conditions. Secular communities developed much later. Some have varied depending on local conditions and traditions, and others have looked much like communities elsewhere, depending on what inspired the creation of the community.

Chapter 5
Utopianism in Christian traditions

Most religions have some version of a significantly better life, even if it is only after death, but Judaism and Christianity are permeated with utopian imagery. Christianity was the fount of Western utopianism and utopianism is a central concern, both positively and negatively, in recent Christian theology. Images of the utopian past (Eden) and the utopian future (heaven and hell, the Second Coming of Christ, and the millennium) relate to both this world and the next one, not just to some inaccessible past or problematic future. They become images of a better (or worse) life, often as fantasy, but equally often raising questions about why this life is not better now. In the Middle Ages, the clergy, and monks in particular, seemed to live better lives than those they ministered to, and some people asked why that better life was not available to all. People often wonder why churches seem to support the rich and powerful against the majority of believers. Since the rich and powerful can have a better life now, why cannot the rest of us?

The Bible

Both the Old and New Testaments include many images and messages that fed into the development of Western utopianism. From the Old Testament, the depiction of Eden, the worldview of the prophets, and specific proposals made by the prophets were used by later utopians. From the New Testament, the message of Christ and the description of the apocalypse, Armageddon, and the millennium in the Revelation to John (Apocalypse of John) were immensely influential. In addition, the apocryphal books (those books not included in the Bible) include depictions of the apocalypse, Armageddon, and the millennium that influenced later Christian thinkers.

The Old Testament

Eden is lost and supposedly not recoverable. After the Fall, it is uninhabited and the human race is locked out until the Second Coming of Christ, but Eden provided an image of unity with God – immortality, innocence, no fear of wild animals, no climatic extremes, and abundance without labour.

Descriptions of the Garden of Eden quickly became more elaborate than that depicted in Genesis, and the description by the 5th-century Latin poet Blossius Aemilius Dracontius (c. 455–c. 505) of Carthage in North Africa is typical.

> A place there is diffusing rivers four,
> With flowers ambrosial decked; where jewelled turf,
> Where fragrant herbs abound that never fade,
> The fairest garden in this world of God.
> There fruit knows naught of season, but the year,
> There ever blossoms earth's eternal spring.
> Fair vesture clothes the trees, a goodly band;
> With leaves and sturdy branches well entwined
> A dense-grown wall arises; from each tree
> Depends its store, or lies in meadows strewn.
> In sun's hot rays it burneth not, by blasts
> Is never shaken, or doth whirlwind rage
> With fierce-conspiring gales; no ice can quell,
> No hailstorm strike, nor under hoary frost
> Grow white the fields. But there are breezes calm,
> Rising from softer gust by gleaming springs.

Each tree is lightly stirred; by this mild breath
From moving leaves the tranquil show strays...

The Fall changed all this, and labour, fear, and death became the lot of humankind. There is no unity with God, and innocence is replaced by guilt, symbolized by the fig leaf. Utopianism is often read as the desire to overcome original sin and re-enter Eden, or, with sin gone, create a new utopia. As the political theorist Judith Shklar (1926–92) put it,

> utopia was a way of rejecting that notion of 'original sin' which regarded natural human virtue and reason as feeble and fatally impaired faculties. Whatever else the classical utopias might say or fail to say, all were attacks on the radical theory of original sin.

There were actual and fictional expeditions to discover Eden and reports of its location were published, and in the 18th century Eden appeared on maps located in Armenia, because the Tigris and Euphrates originate in Armenia. As a result, Eden became a possibly discoverable earthly paradise, even one inhabited by a lost tribe or ruled by a good Christian prince. The explorers Christopher Columbus (1451–1506) and Amerigo Vespucci (1454–1512) both believed that they might have discovered the earthly paradise in the New World.

The prophetic worldview

The prophets bewailed present conditions, warned of even worse calamities if the people did not mend their ways, and held out hope of better things if they did. This last part was not emphasized, but it was there. As Jeremiah said,

> They shall come and sing aloud on the height of Zion, and they shall be radiant over the goodness of the Lord, over the grain, the wine, and the oil, and over the young of the flock and the herd; their life shall be like a watered garden and they shall languish no more. Then

shall the maidens rejoice in the dance, and the young men and the old shall be merry. I will turn their morning into joy. I will comfort them, and give them gladness for sorrow.

(31:12–13)

And Isaiah said something similar in his famous passage,

The wolf shall dwell with the lamb, and the leopard shall lie down with the kid, and the calf and the lion and the fatling together, and a little child shall lead them. The cow and the bear shall feed; their young shall lie down together; and the lion shall eat straw like the ox. The suckling child shall play with the asp, and the weaned child shall put his hand in the adder's den.

(11:6–8)

Isaiah in particular stresses the lack of enmity between human and animal and among animals that was a standard feature of most golden ages and earthly paradises. A common fear will disappear, and a child will be safe among formerly dangerous animals.

Still, the positive vision of the prophets was vague and very general. The closest thing to a classical utopia in the Old Testament is found in Ezekiel 40–48, which is a detailed description of the rebuilt Temple and the rituals which will take place there, but there is also some mention of the way in which land should be distributed to the Temple, the Prince, and the various tribes. The rebuilding of the Temple, he implies, should be taken as an opportunity for improving everyone's life.

One institution found throughout the Old Testament that many have seen as the basis for a utopia is the Jubilee year described in Leviticus 25, Nehemiah 10:31, Exodus 3:10–12, and, more radically, in Deuteronomy 15:1–18. The basic principle is that every seventh year, the land shall lie fallow and be given a rest. But Deuteronomy goes much further by saying that every seventh year all debts must be forgiven, except those owed by foreigners, and all

13. Edward Hicks's (1780–1849) *The Peaceable Kingdom of the Branch* (1834) was one of sixtyone versions of the subject painted by Hicks based on Isaiah 11:6–8

the passages stress assistance to the poor and fair dealing. The Jubilee 2000 movement to forgive Third World debt took its name from this practice.

At a more general level, Isaiah says that in the future there will be no more war, saying:

> He shall judge between the nations, and shall decide for many peoples; and they shall beat their swords into plowshares, and their spears into pruning hooks; nation shall not lift up sword against nation, neither shall learn war any more.
>
> (2:4)

Jewish writings not included in the Christian Bible also presented versions of a better future. *The Book of Jubilees* (153–105 BCE) said that:

And all their days they shall complete and live in peace and joy, And there shall be no Satan nor any evil destroyer; For all their days shall be days of blessing and healing.

And the Sibylline Book of Oracles said:

> For Earth the universal mother shall give to mortals her best fruit in countless store of corn, wine and oil. Yea, from heaven shall come a sweet draught of luscious honey, the trees shall yield their proper fruits, and rich flocks, and kine and lambs of sheep and kids of goats. He will cause sweet fountains of white milk to burst forth. And the cities shall be full of good things and the fields rich: neither shall there be any sword throughout the land nor battle din: nor shall the earth be convulsed any more with deep-drawn groans. No war shall be any more nor drought throughout the land, no famine nor hail to work havoc on the crops. But there shall be a great peace throughout all the earth, and king shall be friendly with king till the end of the age, and a common law for man throughout all the earth shall the Eternal perfect in the starry heaven for all those things which have been wrought by miserable mortals.

Later Christian readers of the Old Testament stressed both the positive messages found in the prophets and the emphasis on laws designed to encourage people to lead the life that God wanted them to lead. And many developed law-based utopias designed to do the same thing, often, reflecting the prophetic approach, stressing the punishments that would be inflicted for failure to follow the laws.

The New Testament

The New Testament depicts Christ coming to save humankind and speaks of a God of love rather than punishment. There is no utopia as such in the New Testament, but the message of equality, forgiveness, and loving strangers as well as neighbours provided the basis of much Western utopianism and many literary utopias. One of the regular themes was simply that a good society would result if people adhered to Christ's message, with the Sermon on the Mount (Matthew 5:3–11) outlining the rewards for good behaviour, saying:

> Blessed are the poor in spirit, for theirs is the kingdom of heaven.
> Blessed are those who mourn, for they shall be comforted.
> Blessed are the meek, for they shall inherit the earth.
> Blessed are those who hunger and thirst for righteousness,
>   for they shall be satisfied.
> Blessed are the merciful, for they shall obtain mercy.
> Blessed are the pure in heart, for they shall see God.
> Blessed are the peacemakers, for they shall be called the
>   sons of God.
> Blessed are those who are persecuted for righteousness' sake,
>   for theirs is the kingdom of heaven.
> Blessed are you when men revile you and persecute you and
>   utter all kinds of evil against you falsely on my account.
>   Rejoice and be glad, for your reward is great in heaven, for so
>   men persecuted the prophets who were before you.

And Matthew 5:48 said 'You, therefore, must be perfect, as your heavenly Father is perfect.'

The apocalypse and millennium

The most common form of utopian writing during this period were apocalypses, which foresaw an imminent cataclysm in which God would destroy the wicked and raise the righteous for a life in a messianic kingdom. Most such works were excluded from the Bible, and the Revelation to John or the Apocalypse of John is the major canonical example. The opening of the seven seals and the blowing of the seven trumpets described there is a catalogue of horrible punishments that go on and on until the entire earth and all of its inhabitants are destroyed. But after the thousand-year rule of the righteous and Armageddon, or the final war between good and evil, a new universe will be created.

Then I saw a new heaven and a new earth; for the first heaven and the first earth had passed away and the sea was no more. And I saw the holy city, new Jerusalem, coming down out of heaven from God, prepared as a bride adorned for her husband; and I heard a great voice from the throne saying, 'Behold, the dwelling of God is with men. He will dwell with them, and they shall be his people, and God himself will be with them; He will wipe away every tear from their eyes, and death shall be no more, neither shall there be mourning nor crying nor pain any more, for the former things have passed away'.

(21:1–4)

This is then followed by a description of the new Jerusalem, emphasizing that it is built out of precious metals and jewels. For example, 'And the building of the wall of it was of jasper: and the city was pure gold, like unto clear glass' (21:18).

Most apocalypses are non-canonical and describe the messianic kingdom in terms reminiscent of the golden age. For example, II Baruch, also called the Apocalypse of Baruch, says:

And then healing shall descend in dew, and disease shall withdraw, and anxiety and anguish and lamentation pass from amongst men, and gladness proceed through the whole earth. And no one shall again die untimely, nor shall any adversity suddenly befall...And women shall no longer then have pain when they bear, nor shall they suffer torment when they yield the fruit of the womb, and it shall come to pass in those days that the reapers shall not grow weary, nor those that build be toilworn; for the works shall of themselves speedily advance together with those who do them in much tranquility.

The Book of Enoch presents a similar picture, and golden-age messianic kingdoms are also found in the writings of the early Church Fathers. In *The Divine Institutes*, Lactantius wrote that

the earth will open its fruitfulness, and bring forth most abundant fruit of its own accord; the rocky mountains shall drop with honey;

14. The New Jerusalem descending on Earth is described in the Revelation to John (21:16). This illustration is from a 14th-century tapestry

streams of wine shall run down, and rivers flow with milk: in short, the world itself shall rejoice, and all nature exult, being received and set free from the dominion of evil and impiety, and guilt and error.

Thus, while the actual Eden may not be accessible, alternative Edens might be.

Although temporarily suppressed because of its radical implications, the apocalypse and millennial expectations have been immensely influential and can be traced throughout the Middle Ages, when they came to focus on the hope of a Last World Emperor who was to bring a period of improvement on earth before the coming of the Antichrist. Such expectations can be seen in political movements in 17th- and 18th-century England and in the beliefs of the American Puritans and, later, the American Revolution. More recently, there is the American publishing phenomenon the Left Behind series, which includes a basic 13 volumes plus graphic novels, videos, video games, books for children, and related products, all describing those left on earth

after the Rapture – a premillennialist belief based on
I Thessalonians in which all the saved are taken from this world
at one time, through the struggle between good and evil to the
Second Coming of Christ.

St Brendan's Island and Prester John

Two influential images were added to Christian utopianism in the
Middle Ages, St Brendan's Island and the Land of Prester John
from the late 12th century. St Brendan's island appeared on maps
as late as the 15th and 16th centuries, and when the explorer
Vasco da Gama (c. 1460/69–1534) set sail, he carried letters to
Prester John, so both figured in the Christian imagination for
centuries.

As Ireland was Christianized, traditional voyage tales called
Immrama were themselves Christianized or replaced with
Christian parables using the same form. The most famous was the
'Voyage of St Brendan', possibly written as early as 800, which
exists in a number of varying versions in different languages. In
what may be the earliest version, Brendan and a few of his monks
seek the Promised Land of the Saints, which is presented in quite
austere terms. In other, much more elaborate, versions, Brendan
and his monks visit Paradise, the entrance to which is guarded by
dragons and a great sword, but God's messenger welcomes them
and admits them to Paradise, where:

> Those who live there will experience no hardship, and harsh winds
> will be unknown, as will heat and cold, affliction and hunger, thirst
> and privation. There will be a plentiful supply of whatever one
> desires and everyone will be certain they will not lose what they want
> most; it will be there at all times and always ready.

The other great medieval tale, the land of Prester John, became one
of the great myths of the late Middle Ages. It was supposedly visited
by John Mandeville and described in *The Travels of Sir John*

Mandeville (1499), together with many real and fanciful places, such as a community of Amazons and one of monsters. Many explorers set out to find it; many reported back that they had. Found or not, the basic characteristics of Prester John's land remained roughly the same. Prester John was the essence of the holy, Christian ruler; the land he ruled was one where a true Christian could lead a fully Christian life, something not possible elsewhere. This fully Christian life has to be a utopia. The life could not be perfect because perfection must await the millennium, but it could be much better lived under a good Christian prince than under any other regime. One literature of the time came to be called 'instructions to princes' and told princes how to behave to become good Christian princes and thus to produce better lives for all their subjects.

All of these descriptions are point by point responses to the curse of the Fall, but none are accessible to the human race without the intervention of God. Even the righteous do not simply choose themselves but are chosen by God, and this is true even of the ultimate utopia, heaven.

Heaven and hell

The actual conditions of heaven or paradise are not as adequately described as are the earthly paradises, but heaven is roughly similar to a golden age except not as pleasure-oriented. Of course, there is no death since that has already happened. The spiritual existence usually has no need of food, shelter, sex, or work. Unity with God provides all that is needed forever.

The 4th-century 'Apocalypse of Paul', which became popular in Western Christianity, provided early descriptions of heaven and hell that became part of Western culture. Heaven was a typical earthly paradise.

And I looked around upon that land, and I saw a river flowing with milk and honey, and there were trees planted by the bank of that

river, full of fruit; moreover, each single tree bore twelve fruits in the
year, having various and diverse fruits; and I saw the created things
which are in that place and all the work of God, and I saw there
palms of twenty cubits, but others of ten cubits; and that land was
seven times brighter than silver. And there were trees full of fruits
from the roots to the highest branches, of ten thousand fruits of
palms upon ten thousand fruits. The grapevines had ten thousand
plants. Moreover in the single vines there were ten thousand
bunches and in each of these a thousand single grapes; moreover
these single trees bore a thousand fruits.

And hell was horrific:

> And I saw there a river boiling with fire, and in it a multitude
> of men and women immersed up to their knees, and other men up to
> their naval, others even up to the lips, others up to the hair ... And
> I saw to the north a place of various and diverse punishments
> full of men and women, and a river of fire ran down into it.

And a revision of heaven and hell by St Augustine (354–430) as the
City of God and the Earthly City was also influential. Augustine
divided souls, living or dead, into the damned, who are the
overwhelming majority, and the elect or saved. Among the living,
only God knows who is a member of which city; it is impossible for
the individual or any other living person to know. Thus, while a
this-worldly dystopia might be possible, a utopia would not be.

But the image of hell that entered people's imaginations was that
pictured in Dante's (1265–1321) *Inferno*, with its gradations of
sinners undergoing various tortures. The most common image is
one of fire, which is depicted in Dante even though the innermost
circle presided over by Satan is actually frozen.

While in Christianity the Second Coming of Christ might occur at
any time, it was impossible to know when, and no one could be sure
that they would be among the saved. Many calculations were made

regarding the date, and there were proposals about how to help bring it about, but over time the expectation faded for most, but not all, Christians. This situation was simply unacceptable. Human beings could not believe that life could not be better, and they wondered both what a better life would look like and how to bring it about.

The apocalyptic and millennial writings came together in Joachim of Fiore (c. 1135–1202) who influenced, directly or indirectly, generations of later writers. Joachim predicted that there would be a third age yet to come in which a new spiritual state of being would transform existing social and political institutions, including the Church, and thus would be something like a utopia.

The utopian elements in Joachim's writings and in the thought of most of his varied followers was generally a vague millenarianism, although there were many heretical sects at roughly the same time that had differing notions of what life in the millennium would be like. But it was only in the Radical Reformation that life in the millennium became specific, with, for example, Mary Cary's *The Little Horns Doom and Downfall* (1651) giving a detailed description of the utopia to come. Then the radical potential of Christianity blossomed forth and many utopias were imagined and put into practice.

Recent Christian theology

Krishan Kumar has argued in his *Religion and Utopia* that there is a profound contradiction between the Christian religion and utopia. Utopia is of this world; for many, religion is primarily concerned with the next; therefore, utopia is heretical. For example, the Hungarian-American Catholic philosopher Thomas Molnar (b. 1921) wrote, 'Utopian thought is itself evil.'

The theological argument against utopianism is much simpler than the one in favour of it because it is based on the common assumption that utopianism is rooted in the denial of original sin.

The theologian Reinhold Niebuhr (1892–1971) regularly attacked what he called 'The utopian illusions and sentimental aberrations of modern liberal culture' which 'are really all derived from the basic error of negating the fact of original sin'. Adam and Eve broke God's commandment and were punished by expulsion from the Garden of Eden and to a life of toil, pain, fear, and death. Any belief that suggests that these punishments can be overcome by human action must be heretical.

The argument in favour of utopianism is based on Christ's message and ministry, which is seen as utopian in that it was often directed at human problems that could be solved by human action. Theologians such as Paul Tillich (1886–1965) have argued that the utopian elements in Christianity, particularly its eschatological character, are a significant source of its strength. In addition, Marxist writers such as Ernst Bloch have incorporated Christian eschatology into their Marxism and have developed a non-religious 'theology' of hope. This conflict became particularly important in the 20th century with the development of the social gospel movement, Christian socialism, and the serious competition that alternative belief systems such as Communism have posed to Christianity.

The advocates of utopia in recent Christian theology are best represented by Tillich, who wrote, 'I believe it can be shown that utopia has a foundation in man's being.' For Tillich, we are utopians because we are human; utopia is, in the first place, the rejection or 'denial of what is negative in human existence'; and all utopias are devices for representing man overcoming his finitude. Utopia partakes of truth 'because it expresses man's essence, the inner aim of his existence; it shows what man has as inner aim and what he must have for future fulfillment as a person'. But utopia also partakes of untruth because it 'forgets the finitude and alienation of man, it forgets that man as finite unites being and non-being and that under the conditions of existence man is always estranged from his true being'. Further, utopia is both fruitful and unfruitful because it opens up new possibilities for humanity but at the same time suggests that things that are impossible are in fact possible. It is powerful because it 'is able to transform the given'. It is impotent because 'it leads inevitably to disillusionment'. And he concludes on a note of qualified hope, arguing that utopia is always and necessarily suspended between 'possibility and impossibility'.

In addition, the Jewish philosopher Martin Buber (1878–1965), author of *Paths in Utopia* (1946 in Hebrew; 1949 in English), argued for the centrality of utopianism to both Judaism and Christianity, seeing utopia as the application to the real world of the messianism found in both religions. But he warned of the danger of turning utopia into a blueprint that must be followed.

By providing alternative futures, the utopia challenges the present to justify itself in values that transcend the immediate questions of power. The utopia emphasizes that life is for humans and that society should be designed to achieve the fulfilment of all the people in it.

The oppositional function of utopia has recently been seen in Liberation Theology, which clearly had a utopian vision in its 'Preferential Option for the Poor' and included a form of intentional community known as '*communautés de base*', or 'base communities', as a fundamental part of bringing about social change. Liberation Theology explicitly opposed the support of the rich and powerful by the Church in South America. In doing so, it appealed to Christ's and St Francis's egalitarianism in particular. Gustavo Gutíerrez (b. 1928), a Peruvian theologian and one of the founders of Liberation Theology, refers explicitly to the utopian function of his theology. As Liberation Theology expanded out of the Roman Catholic Church, which suppressed it, into Protestantism, and to Black Theology in particular, it added race and then gender to class.

Today, there are many Christian intentional communities, some extremely conservative, some very radical, trying to live the life they believe Christianity requires of them. The conservative ones tend to withdraw from the larger society; the radical ones tend to engage directly with the larger society.

Thus, the close connection between Christianity and utopianism continues even while many Christians believe it to be heretical.

Chapter 6
Utopianism and political theory

Utopianism begins with dissatisfaction and says that human needs can be satisfied if certain conditions are met. The simplest dissatisfactions lead to the simplest satisfactions and the most basic utopia, still unmet in much of the world: an empty stomach that is fed, nakedness that is clothed, and housing to avoid exposure to the elements. But some critics of utopianism have connected it to some of the problems of the 20th century, such as two world wars and the genocides in Cambodia and Rwanda. In particular, the rise of Communism, National Socialism, and, most recently, Islamism, which their followers believed to be routes to better lives, have been seen by their opponents as the basis for what has been called the dystopian 20th century. On the other hand, the supporters of utopianism argue that it has been fundamental to overcoming the worst excesses of the 20th century, is essential for the continuance of civilization, and is even an essential part of being human. To some extent, both are right.

After 1989, with the fall of the Berlin Wall and the collapse of Communism in Eastern Europe and the Soviet Union (it is still the official ideology of China, Cuba, Laos, and Vietnam), many works were published proclaiming the end of utopia, just as there had been such works predicting the end of ideology in the 1950s. These 'end of utopia' works contended that the opponents had won in the conflict between supporters and opponents of utopia. With good reason, this position was expressed most strongly in Germany. Having experienced both National Socialism and Communism, many Germans were happy to believe that utopias would no longer threaten them. But they also believed that the end of utopia would produce a better life. Not everyone believes it did, and many, particularly in the former East Germany, believe that life was better under Communism because, although poor and without freedom, they felt, not entirely accurately but not entirely inaccurately either, that they had economic security. Thus, we see yet again the phenomenon of appearing to reach utopia, finding it inadequate, and setting off after another utopia, which will be found inadequate. The opponents of utopia see this process negatively; the supporters see it positively.

The case against utopia

> I consider what I call Utopianism an attractive and, indeed, an all too attractive theory; for I also consider it dangerous and pernicious. It is, I believe, self-defeating, and it leads to violence.
>
> (Karl Popper)

> In most atrocities, there's a big utopian dream – a cleaner society, or purer society.
>
> (Richard Mollica)

The most common approach of the opponents of utopianism is to equate the utopian with the perfect. In English, 'perfect' suggests finished, completed, unchangeable – and nothing human is finished, complete, or unchangeable, so the equation makes utopias look foolish or at least foolhardy. The political theorist Judith Shklar wrote that 'utopia, the moralists artifact, is of necessity a changeless, harmonious whole'. The sociologist Ralf Dahrendorf (b. 1920), who became Director of the London School of Economics, wrote that: 'All utopias from Plato's Republic to George Orwell's brave new world of 1984 have had one element of construction in common: they are all societies

103

from which change is absent.' And the Polish philosopher Leszek Kolakowski wrote that one of what he calls 'the general characteristics' of the social utopia is 'the idea of the perfect and everlasting human fraternity'.

Very few actual utopias make any pretence to perfection. Neither Plato or Marx, the utopian sources Popper cites, pretend that they are discussing perfection. Plato spent much of the *Republic* arguing that his ideal state must inevitably collapse. And Marx is explicit that he does not and cannot know what the future will bring, what sort of society unalienated people might create, and his one-sentence description of such a society in *The German Ideology* (1845–6) stresses variety and change. In *Men Like Gods* (1923), H. G. Wells presents a utopia undergoing immense changes, and in it he compares the apparent tranquillity of the utopia to 'the steadiness of a mill race, which seems almost motionless in its quiet onrush until a bubble or a fleck of foam or some stick or leaf shoots along and reveals its velocity'.

Many utopias are like a photograph or a glimpse of a functioning society at a moment in time containing what the author perceives to be better and designed to break through the barriers of the present and encourage people to want change and work for it. Most utopias are better at depicting change from current conditions to the utopia than the change within the utopia, and some deliberately restrict change within the utopia on the assumption that something good should not be changed without careful consideration. Still, many utopias welcome the possibility of change, as did More's Utopians on learning of Christianity, and many others follow Francis Bacon's (1561–1626) *New Atlantis* (1627) in sending people into the outside world, usually anonymously, to find whatever might be useful for the utopia, and this suggests an openness to change. History does not end with the arrival of utopia; change may be slower, but change, and thus history, will occur.

Another argument is that utopianism assumes that all utopias are based on human rationality and that human beings are only partly rational. As Jacob Talmon (1916–80), Professor of Modern History at the Hebrew University of Jerusalem, put it:

> Utopianism is based upon the assumption that reason alone – not habit, or tradition, or prejudice – can be the sole criterion in human affairs. But the end of this assumption is that reason, like mathematics, must command universal consent, since it has sole and exclusive truth. In fact, reason turns out to be the most fallible and precarious of guides; because there is nothing to prevent a variety of 'reasons' from cropping up, each claiming sole and exclusive validity, and between which there can be no compromise, no arbiter except force.

Popper makes a similar point, saying:

> the Utopian approach can be saved only by the Platonic belief in one absolute and unchanging ideal, together with two further assumptions, namely (a) that there are rational methods to determine once and for all what this ideal is, and (b) what the best means of its realization are.

This argument is similar to the contention by the 17th-century English philosopher Thomas Hobbes (1588–1679) in *Leviathan* (1659) that for want of a 'right reason', life in the state of nature will be 'poor, nasty, brutish, and short'. But Hobbes concludes that, therefore, government must be established as 'right reason', this being the only way of ensuring the security that will allow a full life, and for this reason some have called *Leviathan* a utopia.

Popper argues for a process of deliberate reform, which he calls 'piecemeal social engineering', instead of 'utopian engineering'. He argues that instead of the utopian approach, we should try to eliminate 'concrete evils'. In making this argument, he contrasts two types of reason, one which he labels reasonableness, which he

15. Karl Popper (1902–94) was among the most important philosophers of science of the last century. Born and educated in Austria, he spent most of his career at the London School of Economics. His book *The Open Society and Its Enemies* (1945 with a number of later editions) is his most important contribution to social and political thought

supports, and another which he equates with utopianism because it requires a defined end, the utopia, and what is rational is determined by its connection to that end – something along the lines of 'the ends justify the means'.

Opponents of utopianism like Popper often use the word 'blueprint' to describe utopias, a word flatly rejected by most utopians. As the American political theorist George Kateb (b. 1931) wrote 'any serious utopian thinker will be made uncomfortable by the very idea of blueprint, of detailed recommendations concerning every facet of life'. In other words, the utopian argument is that utopias do not create the artefacts that Popper and others say they do.

But the opponents of utopianism are not entirely wrong in that they are describing what can happen if a utopia comes to be believed in as the sole solution to humanity's problems by a person or group with the power to impose their will on others. This is some steps away from the utopia, in that the utopia has to first become an ideology (a system of belief) and the believers have to have power, as happened with Communism in Russia, National Socialism in Germany, and in Pol Pot's (1928–98) Cambodia/ Kampuchea. But even if we accept that there were utopias a few steps behind the atrocities brought about in their names, in none of them was it the sort of detailed utopia described by utopia's opponents. The utopias were quite vague, being specific only in parts, and the problem arose when individuals were given the power to fill in the details and try to bring their societies into line with these details. The Scottish philosopher and economist Adam Smith (1723–90) put it very well, writing:

> The man of system . . . is apt to be very wise in his own conceit; and is often so enamoured with the supposed beauty of his own ideal plan of government, that he cannot suffer the smallest deviation from any part of it. He goes on to establish it completely and in all its parts, without any regard either to the great interests, or to the

strong prejudices which may oppose it. He seems to imagine that he can arrange the different pieces upon a chess-board. He does not consider that the pieces upon the chess-board have no other principle of motion besides that which the hand presses upon them; but that, in the great chess-board of human society, every single piece has a principle of motion of its own, altogether different from that which the legislature might chuse to impress upon it. If those two principles coincide and act in the same direction, the game of human society will go easily and harmoniously, and it is very likely to be happy and successful. If they are opposite or different, the game will go miserably, and the society must be at all times in the highest degree of disorder.

The problem is neatly expressed by the German philosopher Immanuel Kant (1724–1804), who wrote, 'Out of timber so crooked as that from which man is made nothing entirely straight can be built.' Those who want to force the 'crooked timber of humanity' to be straight and have the power to make the attempt are the problem, not the belief that the world could be better. And even Popper has to have some idea of what 'better' means when he supports getting rid of 'concrete evils'. A collection of his essays is called *In Search of a Better World* (1992), in which, although the rest of the book is anti-utopian, the first sentence is 'All living beings are in search of a better world' (vii).

But people can be misled. As Arthur Koestler (1905–83), the writer who was a Communist from 1931 to 1938, put it in 'The Yogi and the Commissar':

> The peak of Utopia is steep; the serpentine-road which leads up to it has many tortuous curves. While you are moving up the road you never face the peak, your direction is the tangent, leading nowhere. If a great mass of people are pushing forward along the serpentine they will, according to the fatal laws of inertia, push their leader off the road and then follow him, the whole movement flying off at a tangent into nowhere.

The problems that Koestler suggests here, in his famous *Darkness at Noon* (1940), and in his contribution to *The God That Failed* (1950), are the problems of belief and the tendency of some believers to follow a leader wherever he/she goes, even if that be to a dystopia or even to death, as in the mass suicides at Jonestown.

The case for utopia

The defining characteristic of utopianism is that it is a political theory specifically directed towards the creation of human happiness.

(Goodwin and Taylor)

I have never understood why the charge of utopianism is necessarily thought to be an objection to a theory of politics. One legitimate aspiration of moral and political theory is surely to show us what lines of action we are committed to undertaking by the values we profess to accept.

(Quentin Skinner)

In addition to saying that utopianism is not what the anti-utopians say it is, defenders of utopianism contend that utopianism is essential, and they sometimes go so far as to define humanity as the animal that creates utopias. Ernst Bloch saw utopia everywhere. In his *The Principle of Hope* (1955–9; English translation 1987), Bloch's analysis of utopia begins with the fact that we daydream, a waking dream in which we explicitly wish for something we lack. Most such dreams are not particularly utopian in that they are concerned with ourselves and only involve others to fulfil our needs or wants. They are more likely to be about food, sex, freedom from work or bosses than about the elimination of hunger, world peace, equality and freedom for all. But the two dimensions are closely related. As the classical scholar M. I. Finley (1912–86) said:

16. Ernst Bloch (1885–1977) was a German Marxist philosopher whose book *Das Prinzip Hoffnung* (3 vols, 1955–59/English as *The Principle of Hope* 1987) is both a history of utopianism in all its manifestations and an argument for the central role of utopianism in political thought

All Utopian thinking has an element of fantasy, of dreaming, or at
least of yearning, for a better life and a better world. And all men
dream in this way, about themselves and their families if not about
society in general or the world at large.

But daydreams do not take us very far, in that they are more a sign
of our dissatisfaction than a guide to change.

For Bloch, utopia is 'the forward dream', and what is 'not-yet' is
central to his understanding of utopia, with the 'yet' being
particularly important, implying that utopia expresses possibility.
Bloch says that 'We never tire of wanting things to improve' and
that 'the pull towards what is lacking never ends', but such
wanting lacks direction, it must become a drive or a need. It must
move from what Bloch calls 'abstract utopia' to 'concrete utopia',
between utopias disconnected from and connected with human
reality. He does not reject the impulse that gives rise to the
'abstract' utopia, in that he believes that optimism is better than
pessimism and that the 'abstract' utopia expresses hope, even if
that hope is disconnected from possibility. But it is the 'concrete'
utopia that is embedded in an understanding of current reality
and connected to the possibility of actual social improvement that
is important.

In a similar vein, Frederick L. Polak, the Dutch sociologist,
described what he called 'positive images of the future', which he
contends pull us in the right direction. Polak also says that 'The
utopia aims at the development of human dignity through our own
efforts' and contends that utopia is at the very root of the human
ability to achieve dignity.

A central issue for utopia is whether a better social order allows
people to become better or better people create a better social
order. Both raise the question of how to get started, with the first
raising two questions, where does the better social order come
from, and whether or not it can be created with the people we now

are; and the second raising the question of where the better people come from.

The better social order allowing for better people is the classic utopian model and is the focus of most of the attacks by the opponents of utopianism. In this approach, a utopia is written with or without the intent that it be used as a model for a better future, with, for example, Edward Bellamy both saying that this was and was not his intent in writing his popular *Looking Backward*. The utopia attracts followers, as did *Looking Backward*, and social and political movements arise to try to put at least some parts of the utopia into effect. Sometimes intentional communities are founded for the same purpose, often with the hope that a successful model will convince others of the desirability of the utopia. This happened in the case of *Looking Backward* even though Bellamy opposed such communities.

Where better people are expected to create the better social order, the problem of where these people will come from is most often solved by religion, and a common theme of Christian utopias is that people practise what Christ taught and, in doing so, bring about a better world. This can start with an inspired minister or with a person who sets an example that others choose to follow, as in Charles M. Sheldon's (1857–1946) novel *In His Steps: 'What Would Jesus Do?'* (1897). Other Christian utopias are based on the Second Coming of Christ, but there are as many satires concerned with the Second Coming that suggest that Christ will be rejected, as in the famous 'Grand Inquisitor' scene in Russian novelist Fyodor Dostoevsky's (1821–81) *The Brothers Karamazov* (1880).

When a utopia is designed as a realistic alternative, it is intended not as a society to be achieved in all its detail, but as a vehicle for presenting an alternative to the present. In this sense, a utopia is a mirror to the present designed to bring out flaws, a circus or funfair mirror in reverse, to illustrate ways in which life could be better, not necessarily the specific ways in which life should be made better.

Because we are socialized in a particular society and to an acceptance of its views, we are likely to be incapable of a critical awareness of our situation, and we can define unfreedom as freedom, inequality as equality, injustice as justice. Dominant belief systems are capable of blinding people to the reality of their situations. The utopian dream attempts to break through the perspectives that tend toward the acceptance of the current situation, and this can be a shattering experience since it suggests that our current reality is simply wrong.

Two contemporary social theorists, Fredric Jameson (b. 1934) and Zygmunt Bauman (b. 1925), illustrate the current ambivalence regarding utopia. Utopia has been central to Jameson's thought from his *Marxism and Form* in 1971 through *Archaeologies of the Future* in 2005, and he has discussed both utopianism in general and a number of utopian texts. He argues that utopianism is positive because it keeps open the possibility of future change, but he also argues that 'Utopias have something to do with failure, and tell us more about our own limits and weaknesses than they do about perfect societies.' And he stresses that most attempts to imagine utopia reveal its impossibility because we are bound by culture and ideology, and this keeps us from breaking out of our reality to imagine anything radically different, even if better. At the same time, he also stresses the desirability of continuing the attempt, instancing the importance of feminist and socialist utopias that tried to imagine worlds without gender domination or hierarchy.

From a somewhat different perspective, Bauman makes a similar argument. In *Socialism: The Active Utopia* (1976), he argued that utopia is concerned with perfectibility, process, rather than perfection, an end point. Utopia is emancipatory in that it can help free 'oneself from the apparently overwhelming

113

mental and physical dominance of the routine, the ordinary, the "normal"'. Later, he argued that the utopias of the period he calls 'solid' modernity do emphasize perfection, which he contrasts with the 'liquidity' of postmodernity. He writes that in modernity,

> Utopia is a vision of a closely watched, monitored, administered and daily managed world. Above all, it is a vision of a predesigned world, a world in which prediction and planning stave off the play of chance.

But he still argues that utopia is a fundamental aspect of being human, saying:

> To measure the life 'as it is' by a life as it *should* be (that is, a life *imagined* to be different from the life *known*, and particularly a life that is better and would be *preferable* to the life known) is a defining, constitutive feature of humanity.

But he does not like the postmodern utopias, which he sees as privatized, consumerist, individual, and lonely, saying,

> Each one is made to the measure of the consumer's bliss – intended, like all consumer joys, for utterly individual, lonely enjoyment even when it is relished in company.

And he is clearly no longer comfortable with the utopia he once advocated, saying that in modernity,

> In the city of reason, there were no winding roads, no cul-de-sacs and no unattended sites left to chance – and thus no vagabonds, vagrants or nomads.

Bauman, who began as a strong proponent of a particular utopia, has come to reject both that utopia and the ones he currently finds around him. But he still sees utopianism as fundamental to human existence, to what makes us human, and that is basic to the case for utopia. You may not like a whole range of particular utopias, but it is still essential that we continue to believe in the possibility of a significantly better society.

Globalization

The debate between globalizers and anti-globalizers is a debate between utopias, both visions of what the future world should look like and how to get there. There are a number of global utopias, or dystopias as some prefer. The best known is the one that ties the world together economically through free trade and the free market. Capitalists and the major world powers are all in favour of this utopia, except of course when it negatively impacts them, at which point they favour protection and regulation. For example, the USA is all for free trade while protecting its own industries and subsidizing its farmers, at the same time strenuously opposing the European Union subsidizing its farmers. The free market is great as long as it only benefits the home side. The utopia is in the belief that free markets and free trade only ever produce positive results. This forgets, as we are all too aware today, that markets go down as well as up. In the utopia, everyone benefits; globalization will benefit everyone economically and will help spread democracy by opening up or liberalizing markets and integrating markets worldwide.

The second global utopia emerges from the anti-globalization movement and is not as well defined as a *global* utopia because it develops out the hundreds, probably thousands, of groups with very different agendas that make up that movement. In essence, it is humanist or humanitarian, although given the involvement of the animal rights movement and deep ecology, the root word 'human' narrows it too much. It is planetary in that it envisions an improved life for all sentient beings or, to include deep ecology, the biosphere.

There are some pretty basic contradictions in this utopia. At the simplest level, there have to be many fewer human beings if animals or the biosphere are to get their due. At a more complex level, the developing world wants to be able to provide a better life for its citizens, which may entail some serious un-development for the developed world.

Empire (2000), *Multitude* (2004), and *Commonwealth* (2009) by the American literary scholar Michael Hardt (b. 1960) and the radical Italian political theorist Antonio Negri (b. 1933) have been both supported and attacked by both Left and Right and by globalizers and anti-globalizers. In *Empire*, they argue that the nation-state has been superseded, producing a 'new global form of sovereignty' that is not territorially based. They contend that what they call Empire is a necessary stage of development, parallel to Marx contending that capitalism was a necessary stage in the development toward Communism, and in the same sense that capitalism was better than the preceding forms of society, Empire is better than nationally based sovereignty. While some of the points made in *Empire* are already out of date, in that it is no longer possible to see the USA as the only superpower with 'hegemony over the global use of force', this only modifies the details, not their basic argument.

They also follow Marx in that they argue that Empire, like capitalism, produces the seeds of its own destruction, in this case what they call the Multitude, which can almost but not quite be equated with the global anti-globalization movement. In *Commonwealth*, they focus on 'the commons', which they define broadly to include both the earth and its resources and 'those results of social production that are necessary for social interaction and further production, such as knowledges, languages, codes, information, affects, and so forth'. They argue that neither should be owned privately or by a dominant state but available for common use, as land once was in many traditions.

It is possible to be a globalizer who opposes the current process of globalization. For example, from a very different perspective, Joseph E. Stiglitz (b. 1943), who was a Senior Vice President and Chief Economist at the World Bank and shared the Nobel Prize in Economics in 2001, argues vehemently against the globalization that is actually taking place from the perspective of one who believes that globalization can be a positive force.

And this raises the final important point; how you see globalism and utopia depends on where you stand. If you still have an income, you will be able to buy certain products cheaper because other people lost their jobs, and that is how the market globalizers see it. But think of the knock-on effect of those job losses to the shops, cafes, and pubs and bars that got most of their business from those who lost their jobs. The owners of the small businesses lose their businesses and their employees lose their jobs, and the places they spent their money are also affected, homes are lost through the inability to pay the mortgage, banks collapse, as we have seen in 2008/9, and so on.

And such things mean that it is much harder for the multitude to see itself as one rather than as competing for survival, which is precisely what the market globalizers want. There is, I think, still utopian potential in globalization, but it has to come from the global anti-globalization movement building spaces of hope, to use the geographer and social theorist David Harvey's (b. 1933) phrase, locally. We will not make poverty history with slogans. It can only be done by not being conned by the rhetoric and instead building oppositional networks which actually do something.

Chapter 7
Utopia and ideology

The word 'ideology' was coined by the French thinker Antoine Destutt de Tracy (1754–1836) in about 1794 for what he hoped would become a new science of ideas. That usage never caught on, but the word was adopted by others, mostly as a negative description of the ways people mislead themselves and others through their beliefs. Of course, the word 'utopia' was coined much earlier, but the two terms have come to be connected, although in ways that can be confusing. The 20th century has been called the 'age of ideology', and utopia has been used both as a contrast to ideology and interchangeably with ideology. For example, when Communism, one of the most important 20th-century ideologies, began to collapse, this was often labelled the end of utopia.

The first person to associate utopia and ideology was Karl Mannheim, in his 1929 German book *Ideologie und utopie* and his very different 1936 English book *Ideology and Utopia: An Introduction to the Sociology of Knowledge*. For Mannheim, ideology and utopia were central to his understanding of how and why people think the way they do, and he was searching for non-evaluative concepts that would allow him to study the subject objectively.

He argued that the ideas we have, the way we think, and the beliefs that follow are all influenced by our social situation. In

17. Karl Mannheim (1893–1947) was a sociologist born in Hungary who chose exile to Germany to avoid the growing harshness of the Communist regime there, and then exile to England to avoid the National Socialist regime in Germany. He was the primary founder of the sociology of knowledge, and his 1929 book *Ideologie und Utopie* brought the terms 'ideology' and 'utopia' together as different ways of understanding the world

particular, he called the beliefs of those in power ideology and the beliefs of those who hoped to overturn the system utopia. In both cases, their beliefs hid or masked the reality of their positions. Ideology kept those in power from becoming aware of any weaknesses in their position; utopia kept those out of power from being aware of the difficulties of changing the system. And both kept the believers from seeing the strengths in the other's position.

Mannheim's practice was to put together articles that he wrote at different times without systematic revision, which results in inconsistencies in the key concepts, but the German edition of *Ideology and Utopia* was treated as a major intellectual event when it was published in 1929, giving rise to both glowing and very negative reviews. In re-doing the 1936 English edition for the English academic audience, Mannheim removed the preface and the very detailed table of contents and added essays and an introduction to the sociology of knowledge. The German edition has no subtitle; the English edition has the subtitle *An Introduction to the Sociology of Knowledge*, and much of the added material is specifically designed to explain the sociology of knowledge and place the revised material from the German edition within that context.

In *Ideology and Utopia*, Mannheim argues that both ideology and utopia emerge from political conflict. He wrote:

> The concept 'ideology' reflects the one discovery which emerged from political conflict, namely, that ruling groups can in their thinking become so intensively interest-bound to a situation that they are simply no longer able to see certain facts which would undermine their sense of domination.... The concept of *utopian* thinking reflects the opposite discovery of the political struggle, namely that certain oppressed groups are intellectually so strongly interested in the destruction and transformation of a given condition of society that they unwittingly see only those elements in the situation which tend to negate it. Their thinking is incapable

of correctly diagnosing an existing condition of society. They are not at all concerned with what really exists; rather in their thinking they already seek to change the situation that exists.

But as the theologian Paul Tillich said in a review of the 1929 German edition, 'The utopian knows that his ideas are not real, but he believes they will become real. The ideologist typically does not know this.'

While Mannheim appears to place most of his emphasis on ideology, he regularly points to the importance of utopia and contends that ultimately utopia is more important than ideology, saying,

> whereas the decline of ideology represents a crisis only for certain strata, and the objectivity which comes from the unmasking of ideologies always takes the form of self-clarification for society as a whole, the complete disappearance of the utopian element from human thought and action would mean that human nature and human development would take on a totally new character. The disappearance of utopia brings about a static state of affairs in which man himself becomes no more than a thing.

Although there were people who discussed both ideology and utopia together, and some scholars made significant contributions to our understanding of one or the other, after Mannheim, the words were mostly used separately. But in his 1975 lectures on the subject, the French philosopher Paul Ricoeur brought them back together. Ricoeur argued that both ideology and utopia have positive and negative characteristics. Ideology's negative form is distortion and utopia's is fantasy. The two positive aspects of ideology are 'legitimation' and 'integration or identity'; the parallel positive aspects of utopia are 'an alternate form of power' and 'exploration of the possible'.

18. Paul Ricoeur (1913–2005) was a French philosopher who is recognized as one of the most significant philosophers of the second half of the twentieth century. From 1968 to 1992 he was the John Nuveen Professor of Philosophical Theology at the University of Chicago where he gave a series of lectures on ideology and utopia and their relationship

Ideology tells a story, one that justifies or legitimates the existence and beliefs of the group and, in doing so, gives an identity to the group. But the stories are distortions of what actually happened, and it is important to 'unmask' this distortion.

The central problem for Ricoeur, as it was for Mannheim, is the pervasive influence of ideology and how it can be recognized from within. As Ricoeur put it, 'We think from its point of view rather than thinking about it.'

Mannheim thought that movement among social classes, particularly by what he called 'free-floating intellectuals', made it possible to understand the situation from outside, and he argued that utopia could be a corrective to ideology. For Ricoeur, one of the functions of utopia is to undermine ideology.

> From 'nowhere' springs the most formidable question of what is. Utopia therefore appears in its primitive core as the exact counterpoint of our first concept of ideology as the function of social integration. Utopia, in counterpoint, is the function of social subversion.

Ricoeur contends that utopia makes it possible to criticize ideology without having to step outside its influence. He writes,

> This is my conviction: the only way to get out of the circularity in which ideologies engulf us is to assume a utopia, declare it, and judge an ideology on this basis. Because the absolute onlooker [Mannheim's 'free-floating intellectual'] is impossible, then it is someone within the process itself who takes the responsibility for judgment.

Ricoeur argues that from the no place of utopia it is our reality that looks strange. As he puts it, 'Does not the fantasy of an alternative society and its exteriorization "nowhere" work as one of the most formidable contestations of what is?' Utopia's ability to unmask ideology by stating that there are alternatives is clearly one of its positive aspects. And utopia's ability to challenge ideology is, for Ricoeur, restorative.

Ricoeur is particularly concerned with how utopia presents alternative ways of distributing power, and he sometimes seems to see utopias as primarily about power, and even made this one of the two positive aspects of utopia. And in relationship to ideology, this makes sense. The role of ideology is to support the current distribution of power; the role of utopia is to subvert that distribution.

Although Ricoeur spends much more time discussing ideology than he does utopia, it seems that utopia is, finally, more important than ideology. But the two clearly influence and change each other.

Today, ideology continues to be used negatively to refer to the way other people's beliefs obscure the real situation, but it is also used by social scientists to refer to systems of belief, usually political beliefs, that organize a person's view of the world. Thus, mostly without reference to utopia, ideology has become a central point of discussion in both international and domestic politics and as a part of the way people think politically is studied.

Ideologies and utopia are closely related. There is a utopia at the heart of every ideology, a positive picture – some vague, some quite detailed – of what the world would look like if the hopes of the ideology were realized. And it is possible for a utopia to become an ideology. The process by which utopia can become ideology is not entirely clear and undoubtedly varies from case to case, but it is likely that if a utopia is sufficiently attractive and powerful, it can transform hope and desire into belief and action to bring the utopia into being through a political or social movement. Most utopias do not go through this process and most that do fail. But if a utopia becomes a belief system that succeeds in coming to power in a small community, a country, or even a number of countries, it will almost certainly have become an ideology in the process. At that point, it will be challenged by one or more utopias, which may, but probably will not, succeed in overthrowing the ideology, but, as both Mannheim and Ricoeur argue, utopias are the way in which ideologies are challenged.

Conclusion

Archibald MacLeish, who later became the US Librarian of Congress, wrote:

> The truth is that there is no substitute for Utopia and no substitute for hope and that the moment men give up their right to invent, however extravagantly, their own future and submit themselves, as the communists and capitalists tell them they must, to inevitable economic law, the life goes out of them.

And Leszek Kolakowski wrote:

> to go to the length of imagining that we can design some plan for the whole society whereby harmony, justice and plenty are attained by human engineering is an invitation to despotism.

While the word 'utopia' originated at a particular time and place, utopianism has existed in every cultural tradition. Everywhere utopianism has held out hope of a better life, and at the same time questions have been raised about both the specific improvements proposed and, in some cases, whether improvement is possible. Utopianism has spurred people to great efforts to bring about actual betterment, and it has been misused by others to gain power, prestige, money, and so forth for themselves. And some utopias have been turned into dystopias, while other utopias have been used to defeat these same dystopias. Thus utopias are essential but potentially dangerous.

And theorists and writers of utopias have become aware of both the power and danger of utopianism and have presented us with ambiguous, less certain, and more complex utopias – examples of what the Algerian-born French winner of the Nobel Prize in Literature Albert Camus (1913–60) called a 'relative utopia' and John Rawls (1921–2002), one of the leading philosophers of liberalism, called a 'realistic utopia'. This approach avoids one of the great dangers of utopia – taking it too seriously. One needs to be able to believe passionately and also be able to see the absurdity of one's own beliefs and laugh at them.

Utopia can be like Greek tragedy. Humanity in its pride commits utopia and in doing so violates the boundaries of its allotted sphere. Therefore, it must confront nemesis, fail to achieve utopia, and pay for its effrontery in attempting to achieve utopia. As M. I. Finley notes, movements for social reform

> turn out not to have attained Utopia, even at their best, and there is an inevitable let-down. Voices are raised against both the social changes and the underlying Utopianism, against the possibility of human progress, against man's potentiality for good.

This almost inevitable dialectic of hope, failure or at least partial failure, despondency and the rejection of hope, followed in time by the renewal of hope, seems to be the basic pattern of social change and is, perhaps, the actual logic of utopia, combining, as it does, parts of both previous logics. This dialectic is part of our humanity. Utopia is a tragic vision of a life of hope, but one that is always realized and always fails. We can hope, fail, and hope again. We can live with repeated failure and still improve the societies we build.

References

All passages from the Bible are from the Revised Standard Version.

Introduction

The opening quotations are taken from:

Marge Piercy, *He, She and It* (New York: Alfred A. Knopf, 1991; UK edn. as *Body of Glass* (London: Michael Joseph, 1992)).

Oscar Wilde, *The Soul of Man under Socialism* (Boston: John W. Luce, 1910); originally published in *The Fortnightly Review*, 55 (ns49) (February 1891): 292–319.

Immanuel Wallerstein, *Utopistics: or Historical Choices of the Twenty-First Century* (New York: The New Press, 1998).

Max Beerbohm, 'In a Copy of More's (or Shaw's or Wells's or Plato's or Anybody's) *Utopia*', *Max in Verse: Rhymes and Parodies by Max Beerbohm*, collected and annotated by J. G. Riewald (Brattleboro, VT: The Stephen Greene Press, 1963), 54; ascribed to the period 1910–15.

Thomas Babington Macaulay, 'Lord Bacon', *The Works of Lord Macauley*, 6 vols (Boston: Houghton Mifflin, 1943).

Alphonse Marie Louis de Prat de Lamartine, *Histoire des Girondins* (Bruxelles: Société de Belge, 1850).

Thomas More's *Utopia* was first published as *Libellus vere aureus nec minus salutaris quam festivus de optimo reip[ublicae]statu, deq[ue] noua Insula Vtopia* (Louvain, Belgium: Arte Theodorice Martini, 1516). There are many translations available: *Utopia: A Revised Translation, Backgrounds, Criticism*, 2nd edn., tr. and ed.

Robert M. Adams (New York: W. W. Norton, 1992) includes considerable additional material about the book; and *Utopia*, tr. Paul Turner, revised edn. (Harmondsworth: Penguin, 2003) makes the satire and play on words of the text clear.

Leszek Kolakowski, 'The Death of Utopia Reconsidered', *The Tanner Lectures on Human Value*, vol. 4, ed. Sterling M. McMurrin (Salt Lake City, UT: University of Utah Press/Cambridge: Cambridge University Press, 1983), 227–47; reprinted in his *Modernity on Endless Trial* (Chicago: University of Chicago Press, 1990), 131–45. The lecture was delivered at the Australian National University, 22 June 1982.

Lyman Tower Sargent, 'The Three Faces of Utopianism Revisited', *Utopian Studies*, 5.1 (1994): 1–37.

Ruth Levitas, *The Concept of Utopia* (Hemel Hempstead: Philip Allan/ Syracuse, NY: Syracuse University Press, 1990).

Darko Suvin, 'Defining the Literary Genre of Utopia: Some Historical Semantics, Some Genology, a Proposal and a Plea', *Studies in the Literary Imagination*, 6 (Autumn 1973): 121–45; reprinted in his *Metamorphoses of Science Fiction: On the Poetics and History of a Literary Genre* (New Haven, CT: Yale University Press, 1979), 37–62.

Chapter 1

The quotations at the head of the chapter are from Teleclides's *Amphictyonies*, quoted in Athenaeus, *The Learned Banqueters*, VI: 268b-d, ed. and tr. S. Douglas Olson, 7 vols (Cambridge, MA: Harvard University Press, 2008), 3: 235; and Diodorus Siculus, *Bibliotheca Historiae*, 58, tr. in Ernest Barker, *From Alexander to Constantine* (Oxford: Clarendon Press, 1956), 63.

Lewis Mumford, *The Story of Utopias* (New York: Boni and Liveright, 1922; reprinted New York: Viking Press, 1962 with a new 'Preface' by the author).

Lyman Tower Sargent, 'The Three Faces of Utopianism Revisited', *Utopian Studies*, 5.1 (1994): 1–37.

Hesiod, 'Works and Days', *Theogony Works and Days Testimonia*, ed. and tr. Glenn W. Most (Cambridge, MA: Harvard University Press, 2006; Loeb Classical Library 57).

Ovid, *Metamorphoses*, I: 89–112, tr. Mary M. Innes (Harmondsworth: Penguin, 1955).

Lucian, *The Works of Lucian of Samosata, Complete with Exceptions Specified in the Preface*, tr. H. W. Fowler and F. G. Fowler (Oxford: Clarendon Press, 1905).

A. L. Morton, *The English Utopia* (London: Lawrence and Wishart, 1952).

Virgil, tr. H. Rushton Fairclough, 2 vols, revised edn. (London: Heinemann, 1965).

Plutarch, 'Lycurgus', in *Plutarch's Lives*, tr. Bernadotte Perrin, 11 vols (Cambridge, MA: Harvard University Press, 1914), 1.

Plato, *The Republic*, ed. G. R. F. Ferrari, tr. Tom Griffith (Cambridge: Cambridge University Press, 2000).

'The Sweet Potato Mountains', quoted in George Milburn, *The Hobo's Hornbook: A Repertory for a Gutter Jongleur* (New York: Ives Washington, 1930).

The slave story comes from B. A. Botkin (ed.), *Lay My Burden Down: A Folk History of Slavery* (Chicago: University of Chicago Press, 1945).

Edward Bellamy, *Looking Backward: 2000–1887* (Boston, MA: Ticknor and Company, 1888). Modern editions include those edited by Alex MacDonald (Peterborough, Canada: Broadview Press, 2003) and by Matthew Beaumont (London: Penguin, 2007). Bellamy revised his utopia in *Equality* (New York: D. Appleton, 1897).

Marge Piercy, *Woman on the Edge of Time* (New York: Alfred A. Knopf, 1976).

William Morris, 'Looking Backward', *The Commonweal*, 5.180 (June 1889): 194–5; reprinted in May Morris, *William Morris: Artist, Writer, Socialist*, vol. 2, *Morris as a Socialist with an Account of William Morris as I Knew Him by Bernard Shaw* (Oxford: Blackwell, 1936), 501–7.

William Morris, *News from Nowhere; or, An Epoch of Rest, Being Some Chapters from a Utopian Romance* (Boston, MA: Roberts Bros., 1890). Modern editions include those edited by James Redmond (London: Routledge and Kegan Paul, 1970) and by Krishan Kumar (Cambridge: Cambridge University Press, 1995).

Tom Moylan, *Demand the Impossible: Science Fiction and the Utopian Imagination* (London: Methuen, 1986).

Lucy Sargisson, *Contemporary Feminist Utopianism* (London: Routledge, 1996).

Lyman Tower Sargent, 'The Problem of the "Flawed Utopia": A Note on the Costs of Utopia', *Dark Horizons: Science Fiction and the*

Dystopian Imagination, ed. Raffaella Baccolini and Tom Moylan (London: Routledge, 2003), 225–31.

Joanna Russ, 'What Can a Heroine Do? Or Why Women Can't Write', in *Images of Women in Fiction; Feminist Perspectives*, ed. Susan Koppelman Cornillon (Bowling Green, OH: Bowling Green University Popular Press, 1972), 3–20; reprinted in her *To Write Like a Woman: Essays in Feminism and Science Fiction* (Bloomington: Indiana University Press, 1995), 79–93.

Ernest Callenbach, *Ecotopia: The Notebooks and Reports of William Weston* (Berkeley, CA: Banyan Tree Books, 1975; reprinted New York: Bantam, 1977).

Chapter 2

Arthur Eugene Bestor, Jr, *Backwoods Utopias: The Sectarian and Owenite Phases of Communitarian Socialism in America, 1663–1829* (Philadelphia: University of Pennsylvania Press, 1950; 2nd edn. 1970).

Lyman Tower Sargent, 'The Three Faces of Utopianism Revisited', *Utopian Studies*, 5.1 (1994): 1–37.

'The Rule of S. Benedict', *Documents of the Christian Church*, ed. Henry Bettenson, 2nd edn. (London: Oxford University Press, 1963).

Henry Near, 'Utopian and Post-Utopian Thought: The Kibbutz as Model', *Communal Societies*, 5 (1985): 41–58.

Lyman Tower Sargent, 'The Ohu Movement in New Zealand: An Experiment in Government Sponsorship of Communal Living in the 1970s', *Communal Societies*, 19 (1999): 49–65.

Federation of Egalitarian Communities, <http://www.thefec.org/ 'Principles'> accessed 10 May 2010.

Rosabeth Moss Kanter, *Commitment and Community: Communes and Utopias in Sociological Perspective* (Cambridge, MA: Harvard University Press, 1972).

Henry Demarest Lloyd, quoted in Caro Lloyd, *Henry Demarest Lloyd, 1847–1903: A Biography*, 2 vols (New York: Putnam, 1912), II: 66–7.

Hakim Bey [Peter Lamborn Wilson], *T. A. Z.: The Temporary Autonomous Zone, Ontological Anarchy, Poetic Terrorism*, 2nd edn. with a new preface (ix–xii) (Brooklyn, NY: Autonomedia, 2003).

George McKay (ed.), *DiY Culture: Party and Protest in Nineties Britain* (London: Verso, 1998).

Jill Dolan, 'Performance, Utopia, and the "Utopian Performative"', *Theatre Journal*, 53.3 (October 2001): 455–79; revised as '"A Femme, a Butch, a Jew": Feminist Autobiographical Solo Performance', in her *Utopia in Performance: Finding Hope at the Theater* (Ann Arbor: University of Michigan Press, 2005), 35–62, 180–5.

Chapter 3

James Belich, *Replenishing the Earth: The Settler Revolution and the Rise of the Anglo-World, 1783–1939* (Oxford: Oxford University Press, 2009).

Robert L. Wright (ed.), *Irish Emigrant Ballads and Songs* (Bowling Green, OH: Bowling Green University Popular Press, 1975).

'The Non-progressive Great Spirit – "Traditionalism in the Modern World"', *Akwesasne Notes*, 5 (1973).

John Winthrop, *Life and Letters of John Winthrop*, 2 vols (Boston, MA: Ticknor and Fields, 1864–7).

Roger Williams, *Key into the Language of America* (1643), quoted in George H. Williams, *Wilderness and Paradise in Christian Thought: The Biblical Experience in the History of Christianity and the Paradise Theme in the Theological Idea of the University* (New York: Harper, 1962), 103.

Nadine Gordimer, 'Living in the Interregnum', *The New York Review of Books*, 29.21 and 22 (20 January 1983): 21–2, 24–9; based on the James Lecture at the New York Institute for the Humanities, 14 October 1982.

Chapter 4

The quotations at the head of the chapter come from Father Sangermano, *A Description of the Burmese Empire Compiled Chiefly from Native Documents by the Revd. Father Sangermano and Translated From His MS by William Tandy, D.D.* (Rome, printed for the Oriental Translation Fund of Great Britain and Ireland/John Murray, 1833; reprinted Rangoon: The Government Press, 1885), pp. 8–9;

and from the Tao Te Ching (80th chapter) as quoted in
Joseph Needham with research assistance of Wang Ling,
vol. 2 of *History of Scientific Thought of Science and
Civilisation in China* (Cambridge: Cambridge
University Press, 1956).

On the proposed constitutions, see Koon-ki T. Ho, 'Several Thousand
Years in Search of Happiness: The Utopian Tradition in China',
Oriens Extremus (Germany), 30 (1983–6): 19–35.

On K'ang Yu-wei, see Kung-Chuan Hsiao, *A Modern China and a New
World: K'ang Yu-wei, Reformer and Utopian, 1858–1927* (Seattle:
University of Washington Press, 1975).

Donald Keene, 'The Tale of the Bamboo Cutter', *Monumenta
Nipponica*, 11.1 (January 1956): 329–55; 'Introduction' (329);
translation with notes (330–54).

Rubáiyát of Omar Khayyám, tr. Edward FitzGerald (London:
Penguin, 1989). Originally published as *Rubáiyát of Omar
Khayyám, The Astronomer-Poet of Persia. Translated into English
Verse* (London: Bernard Quaritch, 1859); an alternative modern
translation is by Peter Avery and John Heath-Stubbs (London:
Penguin, 2004).

Ibn Tufail, *The Journey of the Soul: The Story of Hai bin Yaqzan, as
told by Abu Bakr Muhammad bin Tufail*, tr. Riad Kocache
(London: Octagon Press, 1982). Also as *Ibn Tufayl, Hayy Ibn
Yaqzan: A Philosophical Tale*, tr. Simon Ockley (London: Chapman
and Hall, 1929); and tr. Lenn Evan Goodman (New York: Twayne,
1972).

Ayatollah Sayyed Ruhollah Mousavi Khomeini, *Islamic Government*,
tr. Joint Publications Research Service (New York: Manor Books,
1979).

On the Islamist utopias, see Christian Szyska, 'On Utopian Writing
in Nasserist Prison and Laicist Turkey', *Welt des Islams*, 35.1
(April 1995): 95–125; and Sohrab Behdad, 'Islamic Utopia in
Pre-Revolutionary Iran: Navvab Safavi and the Fadai'an-e Eslam
[Crusaders of Islam]', *Middle Eastern Studies*, 33.1 (January 1997):
40–65.

Simon Gikandi, quoted in the *Times Literary Supplement*, no. 5392
(4 August 2006): 21.

Chapter 5

Dracontius is quoted in Eleanor S. Duckett, *Latin Writers of the Fifth Century* (New York: Henry Holt, 1930), 85.

Judith Shklar, 'The Political Theory of Utopia: From Melancholy to Nostalgia', *Utopias and Utopian Thought*, ed. Frank E. Manuel (Boston, MA: Beacon Press, 1967/London: Souvenir Press, 1973), 101–15.

'Book of Jubilees', 'The Sibylline Book of Oracles', and 'II Baruch' can be found in R. H. Charles, *The Apocrypha and Pseudepigrapha of the Old Testament in English with Introductions and Critical and Explanatory Notes to the Several Books*, 2 vols (Oxford: Clarendon Press, 1913).

Lactantius, *The Divine Institutes*, tr. Rev. William Fletcher, D.D. *The Ante-Nicene Fathers: Translations of the Writings of the Fathers down to A.D. 325, American reprint of the Edinburgh Edition*, ed. *Rev. Alexander Roberts, D.D., and James Donaldson, LL.D, revised and chronologically arranged, with Brief Prefaces and Occasional Notes by A. Cleveland Coxe, D.D.* Volume VII, *Lactantius, Venantius, Victorinus, Dionysius, Apostolic Teaching and Constitutions. Homily, and Liturgies*, authorized edn. (Edinburgh: T&T Clark/Grand Rapids, MI: Eerdmans, 1990 reprint), 219–20.

Tim LaHaye and Jerry B. Jenkins, *Left Behind: A Novel of Earth's Last Days* (Wheaton, IL: Tyndale House Publishers, 1995). There are twelve sequels plus graphic novels, videos, video games, books for children, and related products. See <http://www.leftbehind.com> (accessed 10 May 2010) for all the books and related materials.

The Voyage of St Brendan: Representative Versions of the Legend in English Translation, ed. W. R. J. Barron and Glyn S. Burgess (Exeter: University of Exeter Press, 2002; 2nd edn. 2005). On the Irish voyages, see Tom Moylan, 'Irish Voyages and Visions: Pre-Figuring, Re-Configuring Utopia', *Utopian Studies*, 18.3 (2007): 299–323. On Prester John, see Vsevolod Slessarev, *Prester John: The Letter and the Legend* (Minneapolis: University of Minnesota Press, 1959).

'The Apocalypse of Paul', tr. J. K. Elliott, in *Apocryphal New Testament* (Oxford: Clarendon Press, 1993).

Krishan Kumar, *Religion and Utopia* (Canterbury: Centre for the Study of Religion and Society, University of Kent at Canterbury, 1985; Pamphlet Library No. 8).

Thomas Molnar, *Utopia: The Perennial Heresy* (New York: Sheed and Ward, 1967/London: Tom Stacey, 1972).

Reinhold Niebuhr, *The Nature and Destiny of Man*, 2 vols (New York: Charles Scribner, 1941; reprinted Louisville, KY: Westminster John Knox Press, 1996).

Paul Tillich, 'The Political Meaning of Utopia', tr. William J. Crout, Walter Bense, and James L. Adams, in his *Political Expectation* (New York: Harper and Row, 1971), 125–80.

Martin Buber, *Paths in Utopia*, tr. R. F. C. Hull (London: Routledge and Kegan Paul, 1949/New York: Macmillan, 1950).

Chapter 6

Lyman Tower Sargent, 'Utopia and the Late Twentieth Century: A View from North America', in *Utopia: The Search for the Ideal Society in the Western World*, ed. Roland Schaer, Gregory Claeys, and Lyman Tower Sargent (New York: The New York Public Library/Oxford University Press, 2000), 333–45.

The quotations from Karl Popper come from 'Utopia and Violence', *Hibbert Journal*, 46 (January 1948): 109–16; reprinted in *World Affairs*, 149.1 (Summer 1986): 3–9, and in his *Conjectures and Refutations: The Growth of Scientific Knowledge* (London: Routledge Classics, 2002), 477–88.

Richard Mollica, quoted in Philip Gourevitch, 'Letter from Rwanda: After the Genocide', *The New Yorker*, 71 (18 December 1995): 84.

Ralf Dahrendorf, 'Out of Utopia: Toward a Reorientation of Sociological Analysis', *American Journal of Sociology*, 64 (September 1958): 115–27.

Judith Shklar, 'The Political Theory of Utopia: From Melancholy to Nostalgia', *Utopias and Utopian Thought*, ed. Frank E. Manuel (Boston: Beacon Press, 1967/London: Souvenir Press, 1973), 101–15.

Leszek Kolakowski, 'The Death of Utopia Reconsidered', *The Tanner Lectures on Human Value*, vol. 4, ed. Sterling M. McMurrin (Salt Lake City, UT: University of Utah Press/Cambridge: Cambridge University Press, 1983), 227–47; reprinted in his *Modernity on Endless Trial* (Chicago: University of Chicago Press, 1990), 131–45. The lecture was delivered at the Australian National University, 22 June 1982.

H. G. Wells, *Men Like Gods* (London: Cassell, 1923).

Jacob Talmon, *Utopianism and Politics* (London: Conservative Political Centre, 1957).

Thomas Hobbes, *Leviathan*, ed. Richard Tuck (Cambridge: Cambridge University Press, 1991).

George Kateb, 'Utopia and the Good Life', in *Utopias and Utopian Thought*, ed. Frank E. Manuel (Boston: Beacon Press, 1967/ London: Souvenir Press, 1973), 239–59.

Adam Smith, *The Theory of Moral Sentiments*, ed. D. D. Raphael and A. L. Macfie (Indianapolis: Liberty Fund, 1982).

Immanuel Kant, quoted in Isaiah Berlin, *The Crooked Timber of Humanity: Chapters in the History of Ideas*, ed. Henry Hardy (London: John Murray, 1990), epigram p. v.

Arthur Koestler, 'The Yogi and the Commissar', *Horizon*, 5.30 (June 1942): 381–92; reprinted in *The Yogi and the Commissar* (London: Jonathan Cape, 1945).

Barbara Goodwin and Keith Taylor, *The Politics of Utopia: A Study in Theory and Practice* (London: Hutchinson, 1982).

Quentin Skinner, *Liberty Before Liberalism* (Cambridge: Cambridge University Press, 1998).

Ernst Bloch, *The Principle of Hope*, tr. Neville Plaice, Stephen Plaice, and Paul Knight, 3 vols (Oxford: Blackwell, 1986).

M. I. Finley, 'Utopianism Ancient and Modern', in *The Critical Spirit: Essays in Honor of Herbert Marcuse*, ed. Kurt Wolff and Barrington Moore, Jr (Boston, MA: Beacon Press, 1967).

Frederick L. Polak, *The Image of the Future: Enlightening the Past, Orientating the Present, Forecasting the Future*, tr. Elise Boulding, 2 vols (Leyden, The Netherlands: A. W. Sythoff/New York: Oceana, 1961).

Fredric Jameson, 'Comments', *Utopian Studies*, 9.2 (1998): 74–7. Jameson is responding to a special issue of the journal devoted to his work.

The quotations from Zygmunt Bauman come from *Socialism: The Active Utopia* (New York: Holmes and Meier, 1976); 'Conclusion: Utopia with No *Topos*', in his *Society under Siege* (Cambridge: Polity Press, 2002), 222–41, 251–2; and *Does Ethics Have a Chance in a World of Consumers?* (Cambridge, MA: Harvard University Press, 2008).

Michael Hardt and Antonio Negri, *Empire* (Cambridge, MA: Harvard University Press, 2000).

David Harvey, *Spaces of Hope* (Berkeley: University of California Press/ Edinburgh: Edinburgh University Press, 2000).

Chapter 7

Karl Mannheim, *Ideology and Utopia: An Introduction to the Sociology of Knowledge*, tr. Louis Wirth and Edward Shils (New York: Harcourt, Brace, 1936; new edn. London: Routledge, 1991). The English edition brings together his *Ideologie und Utopie* (Bonn: Cohen, 1929) and other essays by Mannheim.

Paul Tillich, 'On Ideology and Utopia', tr. Steven P. Bucher and Denise Siemssen, in *Knowledge and Politics: The Sociology of Knowledge Dispute*, ed. Volker Meja and Nico Stehr (London: Routledge, 1990), 107–12.

The quotations from Paul Ricoeur are from *Lectures on Ideology and Utopia*, ed. George H. Taylor (New York: Columbia University Press, 1986); 'Ideology and Ideology Critique', *Phenomenology and Marxism*, ed. Bernhard Waldenfels, Jan M. Broekman, and Ante Pažanin, tr. J. Claude Evans (Boston, MA: Routledge and Kegan Paul, 1984), 134–64; and 'Imagination in Discourse and Action', *The Human Being in Action: The Irreducible Element in Man.* Part II: *Investigations at the Intersection of Philosophy and Psychiatry*, ed. Anna-Teresa Tymieniecka, vol. 7 of *Analecta Husserliana: The Yearbook of Phenomenological Research* (Dordrecht: Reidel, 1978).

Conclusion

The quotations at the beginning of the chapter are from Archibald MacLeish, 'Preface to an American Manifesto', *Forum*, 91.4 (April 1934): 195–8; and Leszek Kolakowski, quoted in George Urban, 'A Conversation with Leszek Kolakowski, *The Devil in History*', *Encounter*, 56.1 (January 1981).

Lyman Tower Sargent, 'The Necessity of Utopian Thinking: A Cross-National Perspective', *Thinking Utopia: Steps into Other Worlds*, ed. Jörn Rüsen, Michael Fehr, and Thomas W. Rieger (New York: Berghahn Books, 2005), 1–14.

Albert Camus, *Neither Victims nor Executioners*, tr. Dwight Macdonald (Chicago: World Without War Publications, 1972).

John Rawls, *The Law of Peoples* (Cambridge, MA: Harvard University Press, 1999).

M. I. Finley, 'Utopianism Ancient and Modern', *The Critical Spirit; Essays in Honor of Herbert Marcuse*, ed. Kurt Wolff and Barrington Moore, Jr (Boston, MA: Beacon Press, 1967), 3–20.

Further reading

Introduction

The best overviews are Krishan Kumar, *Utopia and Anti-Utopia in Modern Times* (Oxford: Blackwell, 1987); Frank E. Manuel and Fritzie P. Manuel, *Utopian Thought in the Western World* (Cambridge, MA: Belknap Press of Harvard University, 1979); and Roland Schaer, Gregory Claeys, and Lyman Tower Sargent (eds.), *Utopia: The Search for the Ideal Society in the Western World* (New York: The New York Public Library/Oxford University Press, 2000).

Chapter 1

The best overview of classical utopianism is John Ferguson, *Utopias of the Classical World* (London: Thames and Hudson, 1975).

There is very little on the Middle Ages, but see F. Graus, 'Social Utopias in the Middle Ages', tr. Bernard Standring, *Past and Present*, 38 (December 1967): 3–19; and Norman Cohn, *The Pursuit of the Millennium* (London: Secker and Warburg, 1957).

The best books on the 16th and 17th centuries are J. C. Davis, *Utopia and the Ideal Society: A Study of English Utopian Writing 1516–1700* (Cambridge: Cambridge University Press, 1981); and Miriam Eliav-Feldon, *Realistic Utopias: The Ideal Imaginary Societies of the Renaissance, 1516–1630* (Oxford: Clarendon Press, 1982).

On National Socialist utopias, see Jost Hermand, *Old Dreams of a New Reich: Volkish Utopias and National Socialism*, tr. Paul Levesque in collaboration with Stefan Soldovieri (Bloomington: Indiana University Press, 1992).

Chapter 2

The closest there is to a general overview is Donald E. Pitzer (ed.), *America's Communal Utopias* (Chapel Hill, NC: University of North Carolina Press, 1997).

On the kibbutz, see Henry Near, *The Kibbutz Movement: A History*, 2 vols (Oxford: Oxford University Press/The Littman Library of Jewish Civilization, 1992–7).

For contemporary eco-villages, see Jan Martin Bang, *Ecovillages: A Practical Guide to Sustainable Communities* (Edinburgh: Floris Books and Gabriola Island, BC, Canada: New Society Publishers, 2005); Barbro Grindheim and Declan Kennedy (eds.), *Directory of Eco-Villages in Europe* (Steyerberg: Global Eco-Village Network (GEN) Europe, 1998); and Barbara Knudsen (ed.), *Eco-Villages and Communities in Australia and New Zealand* (Maleny, Queensland: Global Eco-Village Network (GEN) Oceania/Asia, 2000).

On co-housing, see Kathryn McCamant and Charles Durrett, *Cohousing: A Contemporary Approach to Housing Ourselves*, 2nd edn. with Ellen Hertzman (Berkeley, CA: Ten Speed Press, 1994).

On therapeutic communities, see Association of Therapeutic Communities – <http://www.therapeuticcommunities.org> accessed 10 May 2010.

On the utopian socialists, see Keith Taylor, *The Political Ideas of the Utopian Socialists* (London: Frank Cass, 1982).

Chapter 3

On settler utopianism, see James Belich, 'Settler Utopianism?: English Ideologies of Emigration, 1815–1880', in *Liberty, Authority, Formality: Political Ideas and Culture, 1600–1900, Essays in Honour of Colin Davis*, ed. John Morrow and Jonathan Scott (Exeter: Imprint-Academic, 2008), 213–34; and Lyman Tower Sargent, 'Colonial and Post-Colonial Utopias', forthcoming in *The Cambridge Companion to Utopian Literature*, ed. Gregory Claeys (Cambridge: Cambridge University Press).

On utopianism in early America, see Lyman Tower Sargent, 'Utopianism in Colonial America', *History of Political Thought*, 4.3 (Winter 1983): 483–522.

On More's influence in Spanish America, see Silvio Zavala, *Sir Thomas More in New Spain: A Utopian Adventure of the Renaissance* (London: The Hispanic and Luso-Brazilian Councils, 1955).

On Bartolomé de las Casas, see Victor N. Baptiste, *Bartolomé de las Casas and Thomas More's 'Utopia': Connections and Similarities, A Translation and Study* (Culver City, CA: Labyrinthos, 1990), which includes a translation of *Memorial de Remedios para las Indias/Memorial of Remedies for the Indies*.

On Vasco de Quiroga, see Fintan B. Warren, *Vasco de Quiroga and His Pueblo-Hospitals of Santa Fe* (Washington, DC: Academy of American Franciscan History, 1963).

On the Jesuit 'reductions', see Stelio Cro, 'From More's *Utopia* to the Jesuit *Reducciones* in Paraguay', *Moreana*, 42.164 (December 2005): 92–117.

On the *eijdos* at their peak, see Henrik F. Infield and Koka Freier, *People in Ejidos: A Visit to the Cooperative Farms of Mexico* (New York: Praeger, 1954).

On garden cities, Robert Beevers, *The Garden City Utopia: A Critical Biography of Ebenezer Howard* (New York: St Martin's Press, 1988); Stanley Buder, *Visionaries and Planners: The Garden City Movement and the Modern Community* (New York: Oxford University Press, 1990); Robert Freestone, *Model Communities: The Garden City Movement in Australia* (Melbourne: Thomas Nelson Australia, 1989); and Stephen V. Ward (ed.), *The Garden City: Past, Present and Future* (London: Spon, 1992).

Chapter 4

The only overviews of the material in this chapter are a forthcoming essay by Jacqueline Dutton in *The Cambridge Companion to Utopian Literature*, ed. Gregory Claeys (Cambridge: Cambridge University Press); and Zhang Longxi, 'The Utopian Vision, East and West', *Utopian Studies*, 13.1 (2002): 1–20 (revised in 'The Utopian Vision, East and West', *Thinking Utopia: Steps into Other Worlds*, ed. Jörn Rüsen, Michael Fehr, and Thomas W. Rieger (New York: Berghahn Books, 2005), 207–29), which is primarily concerned with China.

On Chinese utopianism, see Wolfgang Bauer, *China and the Search for Happiness: Recurring Themes in Four Thousand Years of*

Chinese Cultural History, tr. Michael Shaw (New York: Seabury Press, 1976); Koon-ki T. Ho, 'Several Thousand Years in Search of Happiness: The Utopian Tradition in China', *Oriens Extremus* (Germany), 30 (1983–6): 19–35; and Ho, 'Utopianism: A Unique Theme in Western Literature? A Short Survey of Chinese Utopianism', *Tamkang Review*, 13.1 (Autumn 1982): 87–108.

On the Gandhian utopia, see Richard G. Fox, *Gandhian Utopia: Experiments with Culture* (Boston, MA: Beacon Press, 1989).

Chapter 5

While there are many specialist articles, there are few that discuss Christian utopianism generally.

On the millennium, see Kenelm Burridge, *New Heaven, New Earth: A Study of Millenarian Activities* (Oxford: Blackwell, 1969).

On heaven and hell, see Colleen McDannell and Bernhard Lang, *Heaven: A History* (New Haven, CT: Yale University Press, 1988); and Alice K. Turner, *The History of Hell* (New York: Harcourt, Brace, 1993).

On monasticism, see George A. Hillery, Jr, and Paula C. Morrow, 'The Monastery as a Commune', *International Review of Modern Sociology*, 6.1 (Spring 1976): 139–54 (reprinted as only by Hillery in *Communes: Historical and Contemporary*, ed. Ruth Shonle Cavan and Man Singh Das (New Delhi, India: Vikas Publishing House, 1979), 152–69).

On Jewish utopianism, see Michael Higger, *The Jewish Utopia* (Baltimore: The Lord Baltimore Press, 1932).

Chapter 6

At the time of writing, there is no general study of the role utopianism plays in political theory.

Chapter 7

The best introduction to ideology is Michael Freeden, *Ideology: A Very Short Introduction* (Oxford: Oxford University Press, 2003).

Index

SOCIOLOGY
A Very Short Introduction
Steve Bruce

Drawing on studies of social class, crime and deviance, work in bureaucracies, and changes in religious and political organizations, this Very Short Introduction explores the tension between the individual's role in society and society's role in shaping the individual, and demonstrates the value of sociology as a perspective for understanding the modern world.

> 'Steve Bruce has made an excellent job of a difficult task, one which few practising sociologists could have accomplished with such aplomb. The arguments are provocatively and intelligently presented, and the tone and the style are also laudable.'
>
> **Gordon Marshall, University of Oxford**

www.oup.co.uk/vsi/sociology

ONLINE CATALOGUE
A Very Short Introduction

Our online catalogue is designed to make it easy to find your ideal Very Short Introduction. View the entire collection by subject area, watch author videos, read sample chapters, and download reading guides.

SOCIAL MEDIA
Very Short Introduction

Join our community
www.oup.com/vsi

- Join us online at the official Very Short Introductions
  Facebook page.
- Access the thoughts and musings of our authors with our
  online **blog**.
- Sign up for our monthly **e-newsletter** to receive information
  on all new titles publishing that month.
- Browse the full range of Very Short Introductions online.
- Read **extracts** from the Introductions for free.
- Visit our library of **Reading Guides**. These guides, written by our
  expert authors will help you to question again, why you think
  what you think.
- If you are a teacher or lecturer you can order inspection
  copies quickly and simply via our website.